activate your
agile
career

MARTI KONSTANT

KONSTANT
CHANGE
PUBLISHING

Activate Your Agile Career: How Responding to Change Will Inspire Your Life's Work

Published by:
Konstant Change Publishing
Chicago, Illinois
agilecareer.com

ISBN: 978-0-9989531-2-0
eISBN: 978-0-9989531-1-3

Cover and Interior Design by GKS Creative

For Cele, who taught me my life's work is a calling
and making a contribution is a privilege.

Contents

Foreword

I remember the intense excitement of my first job. I was sixteen years old, working for an organization that helped build leaders. I was absolutely delighted with the freedom that money would surely bring and thrilled with my newfound capacity to buy things. The impact and poignancy of that role—the first strand in a tapestry that would become my career—was, of course, lost on me. At that young age, I simply could not have understood the significance of this experience and its trajectory years down the road.

There are threads in our lives and careers that weave together, even when we can't see it at the time. That juxtaposition of a need to earn money—while yearning to make an impact or engage in a passionate pursuit—drives many of us to seek and find that elusive "right career fit."

For most, the career journey process provokes confusion, frustration, and anxiety. It's emotionally exhausting to weigh the pros and cons of new pursuits, to trust that our new direction will provide us what we crave, and to take the requisite leap of faith to begin. And yet it is most often in the zigzag that we finally reach our goal. That iterative process—blemished as it seems to be with false starts, poor choices, and emotional upheaval—often delivers, through an amazing journey, our ideal career. If we are mindful at that juncture, we come to understand that each job—each career—all the while, was in fact leading us home.

Most individuals will suffer in this pursuit. Almost all will find the journey arduous and confusing; over time, many will come to know hopelessness and depression. They will feel defeated in their quest . . . and stuck.

I know. I lived the story of an agile careerist before Marti Konstant wrote this fabulous book. The interwoven fabric of my career has included stints in education, food and beverage, commodities trading, psychology, social work, and coaching. I worked at large, prestigious corporations and small startups; for-profit and not-for-profit organizations; and in capacities as disparate as employee, manager, executive, intrapreneur, solopreneur, and entrepreneur.

Throughout my journey, I experienced many moments of doubt. Moments of regret. Moments of fear. *"What am I doing here?" "How did I get here?"* and, most important, *"Where in the world do I go from here?"*

By following the principles of an agile careerist—although I didn't identify them as such back then—I created my own professional utopia. And with Marti Konstant's guidance, you can, too.

I met Marti Konstant through my good friend Waverly Deutsch, an entrepreneurial professor at the University of Chicago and consummate matchmaker of like-minded career professionals.

In an industry proliferating less-than-credible career coaches, Marti is a breath of fresh air. With insatiable curiosity, rigorous intellect, and astute observation, she has sought to understand the inexplicable nature of the successful career journey through a synthesis of qualitative and quantitative research, along with personal experience.

It is Marti's commitment to the sound process of hypothesis, research, and grounded conclusions that has garnered my deep appreciation for her work. When I first entered the career coaching field years ago, I, too, used research and inquiry as the basis for building my own proprietary model for determining best career fit. Frankly, it's a laborious process that can be tempting to bypass. Yet, it's the very gravitas of it—the intellectual thinking and capital—that provides confidence in the soundness of what's been built—and now shared.

I invite you to approach Marti's book with an open mind. Her innovative agile career model is an iterative process with seven key principles based upon the best practices of the Agile software development methodologies. The process, in her own words, is "designed to optimize creativity, growth, and happiness." Emphasizing rapid and flexible response to change—so applicable for career seekers in today's disruptive business landscape—her process will move you ever closer to your goal, step by step.

Through this reflective lifelong process, you will do rigorous data analysis on yourself and your career. If this is new to you—spending time deeply questioning your career—then you are either very lucky or have not yet realized the profound return on investment that awaits.

With my background in finance and psychology, it may come as no surprise that I believe the two best investments you can make in life are in high-performing investments (real estate, stocks, bonds, mutual funds, a business, take your pick) and in yourself.

In either investment, the overarching goal is the same: to achieve growth. By reading this book, you are making a sound investment in yourself. You *will* grow.

An agile careerist herself, Marti Konstant navigated the turbulent career landscape with a dexterity and vigilance that prepared her to seize the right opportunities when they arose. In this book, she insightfully captures what a successful career journey encompasses.

From where I sit today—with over twenty years as a career coach, working with thousands of clients who have searched for their career holy grail—I am delighted to introduce and endorse Marti Konstant as a welcomed colleague, competitor, and champion in our field.

And to you—a soon-to-be agile careerist yourself—I am quite confident that reading this book, then *working* this book, will allow you to weave together a beautiful, successful, and meaningful career tapestry of your own.

Many blessings to you, your journey, and ultimately fulfilling your life's purpose.

Jody Michael, MCC, LCSW
Founder and CEO, Jody Michael Associates

Introduction

This Book is For You

This book is for anyone who can relate to searching for a true north profession. For someone who ponders whether it is possible to generate income *and* be happy. You are not alone in your journey to uncover and sustain a work life that uses your unique talents and strengths.

This book is for individuals who want to remain relevant in the workplace by responding to change with an agile mindset, rather than ignore or be fearful of the signs in front of them.

When you read this book, you will:

- Learn the seven principles of the agile careerist

- Understand the difference between a steadfast careerist and an agile careerist

- Gain insights from agile careerists—stories of individuals who stumbled, soared, and took risks to explore and grow in their professions

- Receive actionable steps and tools to test how an agile mindset will benefit your career journey

Work Life Experiences of a Novice Careerist

When I was seven years old, my father stood patiently in the dark, murky waters of Wonder Lake at the end of the pier, his encouraging voice saying, "Jump." The swimming lessons he provided were put to the test.

Jumping in without a life jacket, I believed I would succeed in finding the surface of the water by holding my breath and wiggling through the water with my arms and legs. And, well, Dad was there.

This was the first of many incremental lessons that kept me safe in the water and taught me a lot about life.

We acquire knowledge and become subject matter enthusiasts through school or training programs. Who teaches us how to work and cultivate an engaging career? In the world of a freshman careerist, on-the-job training is often the only teacher. We are not assigned coaches on opening day. We have to figure it out, often in a sink-or-swim series of events.

Why I Wrote About Agile Careerists

When I first realized this book was something I "couldn't not do" (an earnest double-negative expression to emphasize inevitability), it was a true calling.

I wanted to help workers reduce the pain and suffering of career management. Like life, a career can be difficult, destined to be full of surprises.

While I did not coin the term "agile careerist" until much later, my professional journey benefitted from a system of awareness, incremental change, and growth. Idea exploration and intentional actions were loyal companions throughout my agile career.

The gap between worklife expectations and reality is a mighty expanse.

Yet when the cadence of response to change and periods of fluid career navigation are nurtured, satisfying career narratives flourish.

I wrote this book to help individuals with "future of work" relevance. And to encourage confident thinking and stability when ubiquitous change takes command of the workscape. If your setback was a job loss, as many experienced during the 2008 Global Financial Crisis, or you struggle with change, it is my hope you will put the agile backup systems and Plan B in place to respond.

Are you ready? Let's do this.

CHAPTER 1

The Rise of the Agile Careerist

The world of work is changing. Adapt or get left behind.
— MARTI KONSTANT

Adapt or perish, now as ever is nature's inexorable imperative.
— H.G. WELLS 1866–1946

Welcome to the Age of Career Agility

The airport was surprisingly quiet on the snowy Tuesday morning I left Chicago to board a flight to San Francisco. The black and white highly polished floors in Terminal 1 reminded me the night shift never sleeps. At 5:30 a.m., I savored the meditative quality of the early moments of my active day.

Within thirty minutes, the noise level rose and business travelers swarmed through the terminal. The Helmut Jahn-designed underground moving walkway between Concourse B and C was flashing with colorful wave-shaped neon tubes on the ceiling. George Gershwin's "Rhapsody in Blue" comforted me with its predictable jazzy tune.

On business travel mornings, I imagine the career stories of road warriors as they travel to their destinations. The game includes observations about the way we work, how we work, and why we work. People-watching with a purpose unleashes stories and possibilities.

For two years, I researched the trend of career agility. O'Hare Airport, my home base, was the best place to ponder these thoughts as I made my weekly trek to bustling work days in other cities. At this international center of air travel, I was surrounded by the concert of important work lives, subject to change at a moment's notice.

With my running shoes on and my backpack in tow, I was ready for the day. And ready to contemplate the potential of the agile career.

The Meaning of Agility

Agility is trending.

Like the artful business traveler skillfully navigating his way to an upgrade or a more optimal flight option, an agile mindset is a competitive advantage in the workplace.

You may have seen recent articles referencing agile or agility relating to an extensive list of topics: agile thinking, agile mindset, agile workers, agile career, learning agility, design agility, agile marketing, agile software development, organizational agility, leadership agility, and agile research, to name a few.

The use of the words agile and agility is on the rise. If your boss indicates on your annual review that one of your traits is agility, your career potential is likely moving up a substantial notch.

You might think an agile career translates to being flexible. And you are right. Flexibility as a career attribute, however, is only about 10 percent of what it means to be agile in our life's work.

The published definition of agile is: able to move quickly and easily. The definition of career is: an occupation undertaken for a significant period of a person's life and with opportunities for progress.

I was excited to see the word "progress" in the definition of career. Yet how many times did it feel like a storm cloud was hovering in a relentless pattern over your last job?

When two years of researching agility extended beyond the early morning airport musings, one thing became clear: agile and career belonged together. Just like heart and soul or time and tide. The future of work depended on a new perspective regarding career development. Influenced by the agile software development definition, conceived by software engineers, I created one.

Agile Career Definition

An agile career is a self-reflective, iterative career path guided by response to change, evolving job roles, and designed to optimize creativity, growth, and happiness.
—Marti Konstant

Much of what prompted my point of view stems from personal career experiences. The career evolution included: artist, graphic designer, art director, brand strategist, marketing technologist, technology marketing executive, and author.

The thought-provoking substance of the agile careerist body of work, however, is derived from people and their stories.

There are compelling individual narratives highlighting agility benefits and defining a few agile careerist habits. My qualitative method included interviews and conversations with people who work. I spoke with senior executives at Fortune 100 technology companies, small business owners, schoolteachers, sales managers, and surgeons, among others. When traveling to New York by air, I sat next to a practice director from a consulting firm specializing in learning agility. Their research focused on the correlation of learning agility to effective leadership traits. Lucky me! She was generous during our exchange and offered to connect me with agility researchers at her firm. I grew to understand serendipity, like the accidental airplane meeting, was a function of an agile mindset.

The peek into the agile careerist habits provides a foundation for the stories that will unfold in the coming chapters. My research uncovered the following habits present in the nimble employee or entrepreneur. These self-directed individuals operate in multiple lanes vs. single lane careers and show an uncanny ability to adapt to setbacks and uncertainty.

Agile Career Principles:

1. **Create an Idea Zone.**
   Take a cue from software engineers. Develop an idea backlog or buffer zone for future use, like they do for software releases. Save the pixie dust of your creative genius by writing it down or creating a digital document for a rainy day when you are out of ideas, yet still want to make progress.

2. **Pursue It in Parallel.**
   Pursue side gigs, freelance work, consulting assignments, education, or hobbies. Create pathways for creative thought, extra income, or future job opportunities.

3. **A/B Test Your Career—Test and Measure.**
   Test your interest and aptitude as you say, "Which do I like better, Job A or B?" Move to Job C or go back to a role similar to Job A, depending on your track record or inclination. Give yourself permission to explore as you discover the best fit for you and your talents.

4. **Respond to Change.**
   Acceleration of technology and continuous state of change calls for flexibility and willingness to adapt. Lean into change and make adjustments to your career status, rather than sticking to a rigid plan. Acclimate to economic developments and corporate adjustments by uncovering engaging projects. Discover market and employment gaps you can fill in a unique manner.

5. **Optimize Your Personal Brand.**
   Uncover your distinguishing characteristics or brand values. Package your portfolio of skills and be consistent in how you communicate and present yourself to the human workplace. Ask yourself, "Am I in alignment with my brand values?" Spread the story-driven message in real life and across your digital networks. Be bold and dare to be different.

6. **Activate the Feedback Squad.**
   No one can do it alone. Seek the advice of people you most respect: mentors, trusted friends, and savvy colleagues. Hire a career coach. Learn from others via online channels. Pay it forward; be part of a feedback squad for a friend or coworker.

7. **Think of Your Career as a Series of Projects.**
Think of your work as evolving job roles. Consider
two- to three-year projects capable of building on
your incremental knowledge. Harness the enthusiasm of a fresh start, master the job, and build new
competencies. Become the most eligible employee
for promotion or the best candidate at another
company, or launch your personal startup project.

CAREER AGILITY MODEL

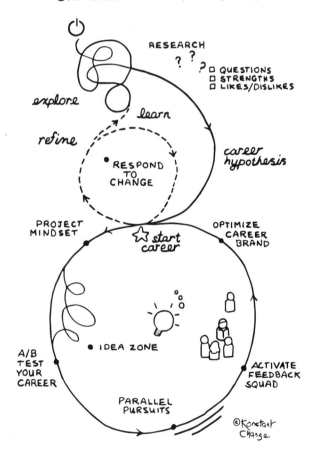

This visual illustration of the agile career principles outlines the perpetual career pattern of workers whose skills and attitudes command workplace relevance. The journey map, portrayed as a figure eight or infinity symbol, will be described further in future chapters.

The Conflict Between Expectations and Dreams

When I first met Nicole Emerick, her easy smile and bright blue eyes accented her confident manner. Her transition from the finance profession to marketing was set in motion as she described her desires and detailed plans.

The switch from one industry to another was believable because of her upbeat attitude and thoughtful actions. She documented her daring reinvention, supplying stories and anecdotes via her popular career blog for millennial women. Her subscribers had the same questions, hopes, and insecurities about their own lives.

I knew she would succeed, not just at marketing but also owning her career path.

Nicole graduated from college two years before the financial setbacks of the 2008 Global Financial Crisis.

Her father, a serial entrepreneur, recommended getting a finance degree because it would lead to a safe profession. "If you know money, you can do anything," he said. True statement. And yet, marketing products like glamorous cars to consumers was one of her dreams. Her tomboy experiences from youth were kicking and screaming for attention. At age five, she was the only girl in her neighborhood to ride a mag-wheel bike.

Her father believed marketing was not a realistic profession. She earned her degree in finance.

When you turn left at the road of safe instead of at the road of desire, the crossroads image can haunt you during times of discontent and searing disappointment. Like a photograph worn with reminiscence, Nicole continued to think; she hungered for her road not traveled.

Although Nicole performed her duties brilliantly at a major bank and was skilled at building relevant business relationships, something was not right. She could tell by looking at herself in photos. Her smile was fading. Envisioning herself in banking one more year, much less five to ten years, seemed like a nightmare. She yearned for a collaborative creative environment where her clever flair for trends and ideas would flourish.

Nicole made a smart decision. Her desire for a creative outlet led to starting a blog and using her time in the evenings to learn digital marketing. While continuing to work at the bank, she took online courses from a Silicon Valley University. She studied everything about the digital space and identified online social media was going to be hot.

She wanted in.

The trendspotter instinct served her well. New social media platforms were emerging every few months. Job descriptions for social media strategists and practitioners were developed in real time as the need for these workers continued to escalate. Nicole's career was headed for a timely course correction.

She made another smart decision. She started a blog about twenty-something young women who struggled with some of the same questions that had plagued Nicole: How do I find a first job? How can I switch industries? What makes me happy? What can I do if I don't like my current role? She attracted hundreds of subscribers who evolved into thousands of community members. Her blog generated income by attracting sponsors and advertisers.

Her creative ideas bubbled to the surface throughout each day, creating an intoxicating momentum that fueled her focus. She held live events, attracting career women who wanted to meet each other in person. She formed alliances with résumé writers who transformed average résumés into attention-getting professional content. She developed her image as a fashionable careerist. With her stylish, wavy light hair and contemporary view of emerging fashion trends, Nicole was an effective spokesperson for her blog turned career website.

Every day, Nicole awoke before sunrise to answer the questions young women posted on her blog. She was credible because she was acting on her own advice. She understood their suffering. The website became a place for inspiration, possibilities, and motivation for millennial women. Nicole felt a strong sense of purpose.

In 2011, she landed her first marketing role, successfully making the transition from finance to marketing.

She sold her website business two years later.

She is now a Vice President and Director of Social Media at one of the world's largest global advertising agencies.

Like the headline testing methods used by email marketers to influence consumers to open the email, Nicole tested career roles. All the while asking the question, "Do I like this role or do I prefer another position?" The answers to these questions informed her decisions for career movement.

Nicole is an agile careerist who has a knack for pursuing a side hustle while working her main job. She embraces the "test and measure" approach to career building and responds to change, making strategic moves at just the right time.

An agile mindset incorporates incremental change over big risky moves. The agile careerist hedges her bets by exploring the landscape on the side, while holding down a job and pulling in the steady paycheck.

Nicole is a millennial, and you might be wondering, "Does this apply to me? I am a Generation Xer." Or, "Does this apply to baby boomers?" The answer is yes. The strategies and habits of the agile careerist are relevant to the multi-generational workplace. Employers also benefit from agile careerists in their midst through higher employee engagement and a better alignment between employee and job role.

The World of Work is Changing. Adapt or Get Left Behind.

The work environment is changing rapidly. The half-life of knowledge is the time it takes for acquired knowledge to become 50 percent obsolete. The half-life of our well-earned education is shrinking so fast it's fading like the last gasp of summer. Some researchers suggest the usefulness of specialized knowledge gained in college lasts about five years, rather than thirty years.

Regardless of our stubborn denial, the unshakable foundation of job security is a myth deeply rooted in our collective memory from a simpler time:

- Before the employer-employee loyalty equation changed

- Before offshoring in search of less costly global labor left people unemployed

- Before the iPhone launch in 2007, when the world's first imaginative smartphone shattered corporate walls for a mobility-yearning workforce

- Before email was overcome by truncated text communication

- Before sending a fax labeled you as an
  unenlightened dweller of the business
  dinosaur era

Exponential growth in technology and our fluid work environments require corresponding responses based on intentional actions, rather than impulsive reactions. Savvy workers who adapt to dynamic circumstances will thrive. Stubborn individuals who ignore the flashing neon signs of change will be left behind.

The Impact of the Technology Wave on One Industry

Breaking down the concept into a micro view illustrates how technology transformed a specific industry—the marketing field. Marketers who disregarded industry developments suffered and put their career advancement at risk. While the marketing profession is one example, you can easily apply this to any industry.

As a technology marketing executive with a background in communication design, I witnessed significant change in my industry and craft. My status as an early adopter of new ideas and technologies filled my after-work schedule with learning opportunities. The changes in the career landscape were stunning.

Consider the state of marketing prior to the internet. There were the Four Ps of marketing to manage when creating marketing plans: Product, Price, Promotion, and Place. Channels like advertising, public relations, direct mail, and trade shows were typical.

The marketing industry trends moved quickly. The industry moved from integrated marketing strategists to 1:1 marketers to brand strategists who set the stage for differentiation as a competitive advantage. Marketers who viewed their experiences as a portfolio-building exercise solidified their hireability. Those who clung dearly to the comforts of repeatable strategies lost their grip.

When the digital age arrived, some marketers believed the core marketing strategies were the same. They missed the behavioral buying trends. While not fully comprehending this fast-evolving channel, many of them failed to adopt digital marketing thinking as a unique way to communicate with their customers. Oblivious conventional marketers remarked, "The electronic channel simply requires an implementation mentality." The reality required a new communication mindset.

In spite of the implosion of the dotcom bubble in 2000, the advances of technology and creation of internet businesses had already launched a Wild West mentality for those willing to mine for gold.

During the next decade, the ascent of social media and a barrage of online tools and marketing software solutions ushered in the age of the marketing technologist. Clever marketers understood the profession of information technology was colliding with marketing.

Marketers who rolled up their shirtsleeves to adjust to new types of digital communication remained relevant. Factors like the 2008 Global Financial Crisis and the corporate downsizing movement beat the steady threat of obsolescence into the hearts of change-resistant individuals.

The introduction of new companies like Facebook and Google seem obvious now, yet there were always those who prided themselves in staying away from potential fads. The expression, "No one ever got fired for choosing IBM," was invented during the twenty-year progression of technology change. It was easier to stay with what worked vs. buying a new software or hardware solution.

Not always true.

The evolution in marketing trends continues. Big data and analytics have transformed the profession. Virtual reality technologies and artificial intelligence solutions are spurring emerging job roles to support the next wave of business development.

Author Nicholas Carr writes about how technology changes behaviors. In his book *The Shallows: What the Internet is Doing to Our Brains*, he suggests the rapid torrent of technology is changing the way our brains are wired.

The next generation of consumers is entering adulthood. Digital natives from Generation Z, born between 1996 and 2010, have been raised in the era of smartphones and multiple screens. They absorb information instantly and can lose interest if messages and visual pictures are not clear and concise. The new advertisers will respond by designing highly visual campaigns.

People who pay attention, adjusting their strategies and points of view to tackle changing conditions and the ascent of new generations, will win.

Why Did the Agile Careerist Rise?

The traditional or linear career path has vanished. The system is broken. Past career management rules no longer work today.

There is a struggle to reconcile the differences while living the work lives we desire.

The relationship between employer and employee has become one of practicality, rather than one based on loyalty. Staffing is fluid. Companies hire people to accommodate demand during a growth spurt. These same companies trim their workforce as needed, adjusting to wild variances in the business climate.

The Current System Breeds Disengagement and Causes Pain

Employees spend 30–35 percent of their time dedicated to work at the office, on the road, or at home. That's a big part of each day, considering another 33 percent is spent sleeping (if you are lucky). Yet we actually spend more than one-third of our time on work. The percentage does not include time spent on a cumbersome commute or being on call, checking remote email, or providing progress updates.

The 2017 Gallup *State of the American Workplace* report states only 33 percent of employees are engaged at work. The disheartening finding is 51 percent of employees are not engaged. When not engaged, employees are likely looking for another role.

According to the report, "not engaged" means employees are "psychologically unattached to their work and company. Because their engagement needs are not being fully met, they're putting time—but not energy or passion—into their work." The study further states, "16% of employees are actively disengaged—they are miserable in the workplace and destroy what the most engaged employees build."

The lack of engagement means many people are suffering, not thriving, in the workplace. Pain eclipses productivity, stealing attention away from valuable contribution. The scenario results in a devastating loss for both employees and employers.

Corporations are actively working to solve the systemic problem threatening their growth. They are creating "people" departments that are separate from HR. A record number of culture management consulting companies have risen to help companies attract and retain workers with the highest potential.

The Shift

The shift started over sixty years ago. We went from the stability of the early twentieth century to a whirlwind of change. The collision of wars, changes in societal norms, women in the workforce, and the rapid pace of technology created a steady rhythm for the escalating drum beat of change.

Globalization and the persistent ascent of the information age contributed to skittish behavior in business and careers. Professional roles have moved overseas, even the white-collar positions we once thought would remain in the United States.

We are in the middle of a massive shift in our economy.

In the environment, when a geological shift happens, volcanoes erupt, tsunamis occur, and earthquakes happen. This creates an imbalance for a time period until the recovery begins. What also takes place is a human adaptation to the occurrence. Strategies are put in place to respond to future events. We evolve.

The economic shift has changed the way we think about our life and our work. Jobs and careers are no longer as secure as they once were.

Corporations accommodate reversals like a financial crisis or a slowdown in sales by lowering wages and downsizing their workforce. Business as usual is transformed into a new normal.

Although small and medium businesses will adjust and grow and new startups are created, these jobs are often at lower wages. Many of the jobs lost during the 2007–2008 recession paid higher wages.

Uncertainty drivers like the 2008 Global Financial Crisis resulted in long-term repercussions still in effect today. The recession forced numerous layoffs, and certain regions and industries continue to downsize hundreds of workers. Another variable, worldwide political uncertainty, acts as the insistent aggravator to our unwanted relationship with instability.

Corporate Survival

There is one universal question posed in every business school, in corporate boardrooms, and in preparation for shareholder meetings:

Q: What is the main goal of a publicly owned company?

A: To maximize shareholder value.

The same goal expectation holds true for many small businesses.

Studying this classic question, I wondered whether workers could apply a similar question, accompanied by a maximization response for the individual. Here is the parallel query for agile careerists:

Q: What is the main goal of the individual careerist?

The answer is derived from the definition of the agile career presented earlier:

An agile career is a self-reflective, iterative career path guided by response to change evolving job roles, and designed to optimize creativity, growth, and happiness.

The goal of our life's work is:

A: To optimize creativity, growth, and happiness.

You might be wondering, "Where is the money?" or think of Cuba Gooding Jr. in the movie *Jerry McGuire* when he goads Tom Cruise to "Show me the money." Yet with these three pillars in check, the money factors fall in line. With a focus on growth, you will build value within an industry or company.

Only you can determine your personal financial goals for success. But I assure you the opposite of these three pillars in your life—too many constraints, stagnation, and unhappiness—will certainly net you less income.

The Employer-Employee Contract Has Changed

First observed in the high-tech startup companies of Silicon Valley, the authors of the study and article (*Harvard Business Review*: Reid Hoffman, Ben Casnocha, and Chris Yeh) suggest the career escalator has vanished. Our career paths are nonlinear, and external forces interrupt career progression.

Hiring for tours of duty that resemble two- to four-year projects is a pattern for success on the side of the corporation and the employee. According to Reid Hoffman, founder of LinkedIn, the company develops much of their talent in this way. If you make progress on your project within a specific time period, you earn the opportunity to advance to another tour of duty. The reasoning is two years is ordinarily long enough for a product launch cycle.

Let's examine the benefits. Productivity and passion are commonplace at the beginning of a new job or at the start of a new project. High productivity and motivation lead to positive outcomes and management satisfaction. Both sides benefit.

Employees are rewarded based on performance rather than the number of years of employment. The idea of harnessing enthusiasm more present over a two- to four-year project captures an effective equation for the optimization of creativity, growth, and happiness.

The future of working calls for a more flexible approach, where the needs of the individual and corporation are both accommodated.

My Road to Agility Started with an Early Detour

My life changed the summer before I entered high school.

I was thirteen.

My sun-bleached hair pulled back in a ponytail, along with my freckled face, hid the impending doom of the doctor's visit. The movie trailers played in my head: going to the beach, attending parties, and sharing secret stories with my girlfriends about what our lives would be like in high school. The carefree summer with my friends was halted. It never happened.

My backbone had other plans.

Diagnosed with scoliosis, a crooked spine, I was put in a full body brace extending from my torso all the way up to my chin. Two vertical metal bars straddled my spine and connected with two leather-covered pads holding the back of my head in place. The singular metal bar in the front and a cast-like structure aligned my spine and kept my hips in place.

The brace immobilized me to the point I could only look forward. Oh, the metaphors are almost too easy. My chin was held in place by a leather surface at the top of the vertical front bar. A circular metal shape surrounding my neck connected the chin rest and the back headrest.

The brace was cold in the winter against my skin and the cast-like structure was hot in the summer. I could walk, but I could not see the books I was carrying, nor could I eat in a normal way. It was awkward in every sense.

I was immobilized from my hips up to my neck.

The metal bars kept me straight and fixed and were adjusted to stretch my spine every couple of months. The bars were like lightning rods for me: for change, for yearning, for the dreams I created over the next three years.

I hid from the gawkers and the mean girls, working on the things I could impact: my school studies, me, relationships with a very small group of friends, and the imagination of my future. Going to dances and socializing in the world of mobile activities would have to wait until I could move.

Turns out, this unexpected restriction and disablement in my life fueled my attitude of "Anything is possible." During these three years, I had a lot of time to reflect—to figure out who I was and who I wanted to be. Self-awareness, however confusing and challenging, came early to this teenager.

I started a craft business designing, making, and selling wooden plaques and key chains to my friends and relatives. The small venture gave me the opportunity to learn about business. With help from my dad, I was able to acquire raw wood materials, cut the wood, sand the surfaces, paint and create quotations with calligraphy, and apply a couple coats of varnish. This was the first of many projects in my career that generated income.

At night and during my private moments of sadness and frustration, I dreamed of movement. I imagined running through a field, swimming in a lake, doing cartwheels across the lawn, dancing to music, and riding a bike.

I replayed my future life movie reel, one where I became an artist creating work like the black and white geometric images of M. C. Escher. In the movie, I went to college at a Big Ten school, impressed young men with my clever conversation, and launched creative businesses. The repetition of my "Anything is possible" future kept me going during the dark times of isolation.

Then I turned sixteen.

The brace came off. In one day, I went from a fixed position to completely flexible and mobile. Something amazing happened. My dreams erupted into reality. I was free to be the person I wanted to be, without the encumbrance of the metal hardware and the inner shame and embarrassment of feeling odd. The wall between the world and me was gone! I released the pent-up energy and ideas into a flurry of action.

I became an acrobatic cheerleader, launching myself into a social hive of activities, and qualified for a dance part in the school play. That summer I became a lifeguard at the local pool. My activities involved glorious, unbridled movement.

I excelled at multitasking and was on a quest to learn and do everything possible. Maybe I was making up for lost time. Filled with gratitude, I savored every moment of mobility.

My studying and good grades paid off for college opportunities. I could move, run, do backflips (literally), and drive. I forged through to the other side of a major setback. My burgeoning abilities to adapt and learn would come in handy as I encountered other certain hurdles in my life.

Inspiration for Agility

Consider the example of a walk in the woods as a metaphor for career goals, strategies, and pursuit of balance in the swirling vortex of a changing environment.

You are in the lush green woods on an early spring hike. You are faced with the task of getting from one side of a fast-moving stream to the other, and you observe there are plentiful choices. Your goal is to triumphantly plant yourself and your hiking boots firmly on the carpet of low vegetation in the forest. There are smooth stones and textured logs positioned haphazardly in the body of sparkling water. You examine your choices for getting to the other side of the stream.

It becomes clear your best strategy is to make progressive angled moves, enabling you to get a firm grip on the next rock or tree limb. Each step advances you closer to the other side. When you jump forward to the next surface, the slippery rock starts to teeter a bit. You check yourself, arms waving and opposite leg swinging to counterbalance the wobbly sensation. Once you secure your stable footing, you pause to assess the next strategic move.

The gurgling water ripples over the pewter-colored stones and on the tips of your ankle-high boots. The rustling wind, another environmental factor, may pick up speed and cause you to adjust once again. The timing for each step establishes a pattern of movement for the journey across the flow of water. Sometimes you slip up a bit, and occasionally one of the leaps is more risky than the last one, but that's OK.

You've got this. Why? You make fine-tuned adjustments to reach your goal.

The Genesis of Agile Thinking and Career Development

Behavior of Software Engineers Inspires the Agile Career Model
The application of agile thinking to career development takes its cue from the software engineering profession. A group of engineers formalized the agile software development process in 2001 and published a Manifesto for Agile Software Development. Some of the principles, slightly paraphrased, include: continuous delivery of software, response to changing requirements, frequent delivery of working software (based on shorter time-frames), and consistent collaboration with stakeholders.

Here's how it works. With the goal of developing useful, market-driven products, engineers develop prototype products, get feedback, and iterate the product numerous times within work periods or sprints to make the changes necessary for market launch.

Remember the days when software launches at places like Microsoft would promote a new version of software with press events and parties? Before agile software development practices were prevalent, software releases were stealth activities involving many bug fixes and creation of popular features. The work built up to a crescendo when the next release was announced. The time between releases was protracted. The promise of bug repair and new features were highly anticipated.

Contrast that with agile practices promising efficiency and just-in-time development. The software engineering profession now delivers needed feature updates and bug fixes for products in the form of incremental releases.

Application of Agile Principles to Marketing

Fast forward to 2012, when I collaborated with approximately twenty-five marketers in San Francisco to apply agile methods to the marketing process. We created a draft of the principles and core values for Agile Marketing.

Just as software engineers frequently iterated software versions to improve the software functionality, marketers discovered they could do the same with marketing programs. The creative process for campaign development can be done in an adaptive and iterative way, enabling incremental feedback. This allows collaborative interaction, minimizing unpleasant surprises between the creative team and the customer.

In the TV series *Mad Men*, advertising executive Don Draper was famous for developing ideas with his team and pitching the work as the "big idea" to the customer. The surprised client either loved it or experienced varying degrees of dislike. Because the creative concepts were produced in isolation without the client's ongoing feedback to work in process, the risk of negative reactions was high.

In the marketing profession, ninety-day plans—rather than conventional twelve-month programs—are more effective. The shorter timeframes offer a flexibility filter vs. conforming to a rigid plan.

You might be asking, "But what about long-term strategy?" Agile methods are not meant to replace long-term thinking, but offer ways to move projects forward with the mindset of integrating the best available information.

Consider the following scenario:

A company makes a bet on a new product launch. Money, technology, and people resources are marshaled to ensure a successful launch. But it doesn't go smoothly. The market timing is off. Should the company pull the plug on the current launch or hope the market will evolve? The company may be faced with reallocating their resources back to R&D or investing resources back to their flagship product.

When the moving parts of the business are managed with flexibility in mind, smart decisions can be made incrementally.

Applying agile careerist habits helps individuals settle into a logical tempo of workflow. It also heightens the feelings of satisfaction that come with navigating change with confidence.

The Agile Careerist Project

The idea of applying agile methods to career management inspired me to initiate a research project. I launched the Agile Careerist Project to gather insights among millennials, Gen Xers, and boomers about their strategies to start and navigate through their career paths. Privileged to share conversations with over 120 global workers, I gained pivotal awareness about the world of work.

In addition to my primary research, I studied a number of reports, books, and articles on careers, workplace, leadership, personal development, transformation, and reinvention. I wanted to learn as much as possible about the agile mindset. Most important, the question "Can career agility be learned?" required an answer, or at least an informed opinion.

Interviews and meetings explored how people work, what makes them happy, what keeps them engaged, and what inspires their motivation. What makes some people more successful at career navigation than others? How do some people adapt to change more than others?

While researching the topic of agility for this book, I analyzed my personal work history. The approach to my life's work employed a hedging your bet strategy. Just like a diversified financial portfolio, my burgeoning skills were treated like a portfolio and it was my responsibility to optimize them.

These awakenings informed my subsequent decisions about my life's work and resulted in useful career navigation habits. I treated my career as a platform for personal development and established a pattern of behavior for my interest in the agile career.

The framework discussed in this book won't erase all the pain caused by uncertainty or eventual disappointments. But it will provide steps to sustain forward progress, optimizing the important aspects of your work and well-being: creativity, growth, and happiness.

Key Findings of The Agile Careerist Project

The project illuminated a variety of compelling insights. The following chapters will isolate the seven essential principles of the agile careerist. If you are curious about insights gained throughout the project, you may benefit from a shortened version of my observations.

A peek into my findings uncovered two different types of careerists: the agile careerist and the steadfast careerist.

Agile careerist behaviors:

- Example: Richard Branson, who consistently responds to change
- Create personal career rotations based on interests and drive, rather than depending on one career track
- Uncover new job descriptions in their industry and invent job descriptions to accommodate their skill sets and interests
- Adapt to change and are flexible, rather than avoiding change
- Possess and cultivate curiosity and resilience
- Believe in do-it-yourself career management, rather than relying on corporate development or human resources
- Follow and leverage industry trends to stay ahead of the curve for the next role
- Seek out advice and feedback from mentors (formal and informal)
- View careers as a series of projects
- Optimize skills to grow professionally; seek out additional roles within the same company or reach out to a new company for the next stage of growth
- Value creativity, growth, and happiness in their life's work

- A/B test jobs on a regular basis, testing and measuring personal aptitude and interest with each new role
- Pursue jobs and interests in parallel with the main job
- Build a personal work portfolio, fortifying skill sets with each new role
- Build and manage personal brands; communicate and package who they are, how they are different, and why it's important
- Are highly productive workers who achieve happiness, gain access to new opportunities, and attain an impressive number of accomplishments
- May stay with one company for many years, switch jobs at strategic intervals, or start their own businesses
- Get bored with work that does not reflect a growth pattern
- Reinvent career paths, switching lanes from one career track to another

Steadfast careerist behaviors:

- Example: Kay Whitmore of Kodak, who denied the digital trend in photography, an attitude that contributed to the company's demise
- Pursue job loyalty, rather than adventure and risk
- Prefer predictable environments and circumstances

- Struggle with uncertainty and avoid change rather than adapt to change
- Work within their capabilities, rather than accumulate new skills
- Require structure and direction from organizations for a career path, rather than adopt self-direction
- Are often blindsided by trends that lead to uncertainty and job loss
- As Michele Wucker points out in her book, *The Gray Rhino*, this group ignores obvious dangers and does not act on them, in spite of the warning signs
- Typically lack a Plan B
- Stay at roles longer than agile careerists with intention of ensuring job security

As shown in the diagram on the following page, all workers fall on a spectrum between agile and steadfast. Steadfast careerists require significant structure, are rules-driven, and prefer direction. Agile careerists are inherently self-directed. Higher agility scale scores correlate to a higher comfort level with uncertainty and change and lead to a state of continuous career progress.

We learned earlier from Nicole Emerick's career that dissatisfaction can lead to a desired change. Mid-career can be the time when questions arise. "How did I get here? or "This isn't what I thought it was going to be like," are sentiments that can lead to confusion and stop workers in their tracks. Agile careerists pose similar questions but do not stay in a role lacking opportunity or growth.

CAREER AGILITY SPECTRUM

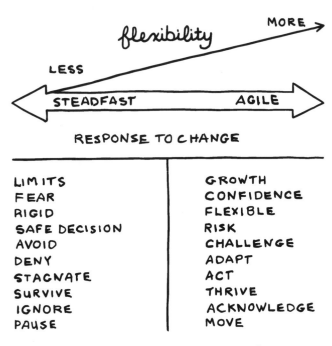

flexibility

MORE →

LESS

← STEADFAST   AGILE →

RESPONSE TO CHANGE

LIMITS	GROWTH
FEAR	CONFIDENCE
RIGID	FLEXIBLE
SAFE DECISION	RISK
AVOID	CHALLENGE
DENY	ADAPT
STAGNATE	ACT
SURVIVE	THRIVE
IGNORE	ACKNOWLEDGE
PAUSE	MOVE

©Konstant
Change

Technology influences have altered the job roles required to grow companies. Companies are becoming flatter in their management structure, instead of hierarchical. The astute navigators write their own job descriptions to better address corporate needs.

The conventional rules of career navigation are in flux, but one rule is evergreen: a well-nurtured network ensures future opportunities. Agile thinkers stay in touch with the people in their orbit and do not wait until they lose their jobs to ignite communication.

Adopting an agile mindset is an empowered first response to the torrent of change. The rise of the agile careerist puts the employee in charge. The human resources department is just that: a resource. The best person to direct your career is you.

Because an agile careerist optimizes for creativity, growth, and happiness, she is more likely to be in a role suited to her talents and interests.

When I ask the question in the agile careerist interviews, "What are you most proud of regarding your life's work?" I typically observe a beaming smile and a satisfied faraway look in their eyes. The earnest recollection tells me the spectacular moment of accomplishment was beneficial to their companies, their bosses, and their departments.

The deposit into the self-esteem bucket is still brimming years later. These storied moments happen when workers' talents and interests are in alignment with the company goals.

Summary

A position at the helm of your own ship leads to a mindset claiming, "I've got this," and "I can do this," rather than "I don't know whether I can take one more day of this [fill in the blank] job!"

Careers are riddled with change. Life creates unexpected personal circumstances. The economy crashes. Jobs are downsized. Office politics get in the way. Our work lives are never quite what we imagined. We don't always have the command of the reins during our career journey. It can feel like someone else is in charge.

The agile careerist model tackles the evolution of these moving parts: people, companies, technology, and job roles.

Agile Career Framework Mitigates Pain and Suffering
The agile careerist framework was developed to eliminate suffering that exists when a person stays in a role not aligned with his or her talents and interests. Don't you hate when that happens? Shifting the responsibility of professional development to the individual instead of the employer is a step toward self-direction and empowerment. This is in contrast to reliance on the structure of corporate employee management.

The agile careerist definition merits a quick review:

> An agile career is a self-reflective, iterative career path guided by response to change, evolving job roles, and designed to optimize creativity, growth, and happiness.

Individual focus on the optimization of personal creativity, growth, and happiness complements the corporation's focus on the bottom line of productivity and profit.

I believe career agility can be learned. As a valuable form of career currency, it is the cost of entry for sustained career relevance in the workplace of the future.

Next Steps
To understand how to be agile, you first need to understand what motivates you. Whether you are perfectly content in your current job, or wonder whether there is something better for you in your career, this is an effective exercise:

1. Discover what makes your heart sing. Think back to a time when you were happy in your work, when you were in the zone of doing your best work. What were you doing? The answer is not

necessarily your job role, but a feeling you experienced regarding your work. Maybe it was a time when you were working in a team or launching a new product. Write your response to this. If you prefer a visual exercise, create a vision board for yourself. The important thing is to explore what makes you feel creative, what makes you feel productive, and what makes you happy. Answer these questions: How did you spend your time when you were eleven years old? What did you like to do? What were you good at?

2. Describe your proudest moment in your life's work.

3. Explore your work environment to determine whether there is a project utilizing the skills and experiences described above that differ from your current role. Gather research about opportunities outside of your current workplace that speak to your skills and interests. Make a list of the opportunities around you that are aligned with your talents.

CHAPTER 2

Principle One:
Create an Idea Zone

I begin with an idea and then it becomes something else.
— PABLO PICASSO

Serendipity on the Lakefront Running Path

At six o'clock on a chilly Chicago morning in May 2013, I bolted out the front door to meet with a group of curiously enthusiastic strangers on the lakefront running path. The seven global travelers had responded to a tweet beckoning joggers attending a three-day conference to embrace the day with a morning run.

With the glistening reflection of the lake to the east and the stunning view of Chicago's architecture to the west, I felt proud to host my fellow conference attendees during my typical morning ritual.

As an introvert with occasional extrovert behaviors, I was elated to meet and socialize with optimistic, like-minded morning people. Customary conference interaction among participants happens after hours, like singing in a karaoke bar or partaking in the gregarious nightlife of the city. Not my style.

Running tights, performance t-shirts, and cozy fleece vests comprise the dress code where I feel most like me. And it wouldn't be complete without the baseball cap and pony-tail that tame the flyaway hair caused by the winds off Lake Michigan.

The most appealing experiences of a group athletic activity with an eclectic mix of people are the conversations happening when the sweat starts to trickle and the endorphins kick in. When there is no agenda, when the communication is real. With our unadorned faces and athletic clothing, I felt right at home with the candid icebreaker chats.

Drew Marshall, one of my jogging mates, noticed my pace was slowing down at the turnaround point near the Field Museum. He graciously reduced his tempo to match my stride. As we continued our dialogue in the cool spring air, it was clear I was in the presence of an agile careerist. On a scale of one to ten, where ten indicates highly agile, Drew ranked at the top of the scale.

Here is his story.

How Ideas Morph into Action

Drew Marshall, a Gen Xer, is an idea machine.

I recently caught up with Drew at an Urban Café in Manhattan near Times Square. In the previous twenty-four hours, he had traveled from Mexico City to New York. His stamina was impressive for sure, but I was also taken by his present, in-the-moment demeanor as we discussed his agile career.

Just like the time he slowed his pace to accompany me on our morning run, he approached his communication in a humble way, listening carefully. He has a gift for putting people at ease, a useful skill in the workplace.

With his closely shaven head and fashionable specs, he has the appearance of a smart-looking architect. He expresses brainy anecdotes through genuine sharing of his distinctive lens on the world. With the style of a creative professional and the shrewd manner of a business strategist, Drew works as an innovation consultant.

The alleyways and footpaths of Drew's career journey were brimming with ideas. His exposure to work started quite young.

Drew's early upbringing could best be described by his fortunate experiences as an apprentice in a charming hamlet south of Sydney, Australia. He lived on a cul-de-sac in an area known as Sutherland Shire. The idyllic Sydney suburb in New South Wales is set between surfer haven beaches and rugged sea cliffs to the east and the lush Royal National Park to the west.

The Protestant work ethic mentality summarized the pulse of the lively community. Sacrifices and hours outside the work window were customary to sustain successful interdependent local businesses. He started as an industrious paperboy delivering newspapers with a rustic wheelbarrow throughout his town. Every family in the neighborhood managed one small business representing the heart and contributions of each family.

In summer, he worked as an apprentice to small and medium-sized companies in the entrepreneurial business haven representing a range of enterprises: display case manufacturer, gourmet chocolatier, auto supply store, shoe factory, and architecture firm, to name a few. He worked on the factory floors, in the offices, and at retail counters, acquiring a variety of flexible work habits.

He was attracted to two things: systems and people. Like a board game strategist, he could see the patterns and unique styles of the hardworking entrepreneurs and their businesses. He dissected the stories of the ups and downs of their entrepreneurial experiences, analyzing the difference between logical success and painful struggle.

His mother, a prenatal physiotherapist, was an entrepreneur who taught childbirth preparation classes in the home, helping to bring children into the world. His father owned a local store, a place he managed when forced into early retirement by a global conglomerate. People with perseverance surrounded Drew. They taught him how to stick with it through the difficult times and how to find the assured path to prosperity.

Drew collects ideas the way some people collect baseball cards. During his apprenticeship years, he accumulated concepts about how to improve the employee and customer experiences. After receiving a master's degree in whole systems design in Seattle, he applied concepts of regenerative systems to the cultivation and development of human beings.

With a perceptive eye on human performance since his early days in the entrepreneurial neighborhood of the shire, Drew became a student of human behavior in the workplace.

When systems were aligned, Drew reasoned, the organization hummed with the production of improved products and motivated employees. At the center of Drew's idea factory is the ability to observe patterns and systems from one discipline and to reframe the touchstone idea for another company or industry. He mastered this comparative technique while helping companies solve critical problems.

As a chief innovation officer, he created a vast repository of themes around service, systems design, innovation, leadership, organizational change, and, most essential, respectful people management. When challenges overwhelmed his personal principles, Drew took a deep breath and inventoried his myriad ideas for hidden solutions.

An idea person cannot be conquered.

As a fundamental capability, Drew learned how to motivate people around a shared goal. He cringed with concern when he witnessed dictatorial or dominating styles of management. His instinctive style is to meet individuals on their terms and truly understand what drives them in their work environment.

Inspirational, motivated people create the yellow brick road to innovation.

Yet regardless of how well the agile career navigator manages his career, toxic bosses can upstage an otherwise ideal work environment. When this happened to Drew, he smoothed his bumpy ride through the road to entrepreneurship as an innovation consultant.

Speaking of ideas, sometimes the best idea is to leave.

Whenever one of the core pillars of the agile career— creativity, growth, or happiness—is at risk, it's time to make adjustments.

Idea Derivatives

When Drew started his own company, he discovered his genuine talent as an external influencer within internal teams. His ability to stimulate ideas within teams and departments results in innovative product creations and powerful people solutions.

His favorite words to live by are:

Do what you love in service of people
who love what you do.
—*Steve Farber, founder of Extreme Leadership,*
best-selling author, speaker, and executive coach

From the early days of learning in Sutherland Shire to his current work as an innovation consultant in the United States, his flair for perpetual idea flow solidifies his worth in the job market.

His Idea Zone is a place to collect and connect.

With his high-frequency radar scanning the world around him, Drew's transponder captures ideas sparking his imagination. He divides the content into two sections: his own personal development and beneficial topics for his clients. By gathering material over time via links, images, and documents, he creates a resource reserve that he nurtures for further inspiration. These ideas accumulate in a fertile field, ready to bloom into valuable concepts for immediate application or future consideration.

The Idea Zone is the ideal platform to achieve Drew's true inclination to learn and grow.

The Idea Zone Principle

Let's take a moment to focus on this creative principle.

Principle One: Create an Idea Zone

Take a cue from software engineers. Develop an idea backlog or buffer zone for future use, similar to the software release process. Save the pixie dust of your creative genius by writing it down or creating a digital document. Review on a rainy day when you are out of ideas, yet still want to make progress.

Career management is a mighty project requiring mighty big shoulders. Filled with complexity and nuance, a career is one of the most important long-term projects of your life. Unfortunately, career ideation and career development are not required reading in high school or college.

Learning on the job resembles a trial by fire experience, startling participants with a series of test projects. Phrases like "jump into the deep end" or "sink or swim" summarize work situations requiring self-reliance and a quick learning aptitude. Idea generation and "in the moment" problem solving define one's true character.

There is no syllabus and there are no shortcuts. Just the anxious moments near the top of the roller coaster. When you hear the clicking and clanking of the chains, you determine whether you are a screamer with your hands held high to heighten the exhilarating drop, or you close your eyes and hold your breath. The only way through it, however, is to fully absorb the moments of certain uncertainty.

We all leap into career land with a similar level of inexperience. We hear the phrases of the career lottery winners who dispense logical advice, err . . . platitudes, like: Follow your dreams. Do what you love and the money will follow. Do what you love and you will never work a day in your life. These admonitions become irritating and provide meager comfort when we are mired in the muck of our career's blurry vision.

The ideas about what we might be when we grow up are buried in a mind reel that plays more clearly between the ages of five and ten. In adulthood, all bets are off.

When you think back on that inventive time of your life, what do you remember? The career choices were quite simple: fireman, dancer, doctor, world traveler, artist, or pilot.

Not many five-year-olds choose lawyer or accountant. Yet somewhere between ten years old and college age, an abundant number of young adults choose the pragmatic professional route that assures adequate accumulation of wealth. The benchmark for wealth or "enough money" is different for all of us, resulting in choices ranging from social worker to investment banker.

While researching this book, when I posed the question, "Did you ever imagine what your day-to-day work environment would be like prior to your work life?" 85 percent of the research participants said no. They simply jumped in and figured it out later. How did you land your first job?

Because experience is a necessary part of defining dreams for our life's work, jumping in with the intent to learn is precisely what is needed. The same holds true for picking college majors. Until you accumulate a body of knowledge through experience, it's difficult to know what you don't know until you have collected enough data points.

Diving in leads to immersion and first-hand experience. Brains are ripe with creativity once people are able to compare and contrast experiences. The serendipity of unexpected connections assembles the foundation for innovative thinking and evaluation. "Do I like this job or the one in the next department?" The intentional experimentation prompts choices we may never have considered.

Capture the Idea Flow

Ideas are dynamic. Like the pithy messages of a fast moving Twitter feed, they can disappear like a firefly on a dark summer night.

To benefit from ideas, it's essential to capture them the moment they materialize. Collecting ideas with reckless abandon, without judgment or opinion, will inspire you. Writing them down or creating a story to remember them will build up a reserve that will be helpful when you are staring at a blank screen.

Store the inspiring thoughts that descend upon you when you are running, walking, doing the dishes, or in the half dream state before the morning alarm jolts you to attention. Keep these gems alive over time by building upon them, sharing them, securing feedback, and analyzing them.

Learn from software engineers. Develop an idea backlog for future use, like they do for software releases.

The Idea Zone is a place to keep a list of uncensored ideas about your career and fresh solutions for your projects. Whether the zone is an Evernote document or is hand written in a cherished journal, create a convenient place for idea capture. The rich idea repository protects your innovative thoughts, preserving them for easy access.

In agile software development, this term is called the idea backlog. This list is actively monitored for relevance until it is needed for an update or future version of a product.

Drew Marshall writes everything down. "It provides clarity," he says, and "helps to prioritize and get feedback from work buddies or trusted advisors." He uses the online note-taking application Evernote to accommodate his various device input habits and relies on the file-hosting service Dropbox for storing ideas in a research folder. "The ideas percolate in my head for a time, but I find if I don't capture them, they flee." He jokingly refers to himself as a digital hoarder.

The Idea Zone for agile careerists is an innovation engine for your career. Whether you use a notebook or a digital storage tool, tracking ideas for project and career design will keep you focused on growth and what is possible for your future.

IDEA ZONE

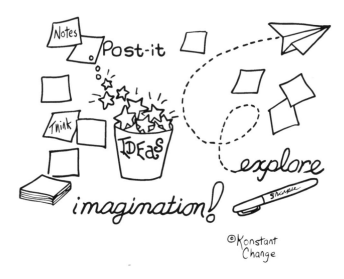

Solutions and projects derived from collaborative idea exchanges drive personal growth and are essential for getting noticed. A fresh supply of ideas for ongoing work projects is a clever way to earn a reputation as the problem solver on the team. Coming to the table ready to brainstorm will impress the people in power when it is time for a review, raise, or promotion.

Storytelling as Learning Currency

While collecting ideas is an effective daily habit, the application of ideas is where magic steps out of the genie bottle into the universe of plentiful potential. Storytelling is the framework that unlocks the receptor of understanding in our brains.

Drew said it best when he shared, "Stories are the universal currency of learning. I find gathering story-form examples of content I wish to remember and repurpose is key to transporting them between bodies of knowledge." He believes data from one industry may be relevant for another, but organizations are unable to see this. "The story and the lesson within the data, however, are universally applicable."

Ideas and Happiness

Have you ever had a bad day at work? OK, maybe it's been an entire month or year. The benefit of a top-of-mind view into your gold mine of inspired thought is an immediate attitude adjustment.

Maybe you're not ready to move on an idea right away. A creative spark, however, can infuse you with optimistic energy when a toxic situation festers with an impatient force. A rough workday can devolve into a horror film filled with bad bosses and projects gone wrong.

Ideas pave the way toward choices when lack of ideas can lure you into a murky corner. The reserve weapons of the work warriors are the creative daydreams and happy thoughts that stand by as reinforcements for the weary worker.

In the movie *It's a Wonderful Life*, Clarence, an angel waiting to earn his wings, is informed George Bailey needs help. Clarence asks, "Is he sick?" A senior angel responds, "No, worse. He's discouraged." The weight of discouragement can color our world with hopeless shades of gray. Ideas propagate colorful thinking and encouraging points of view in times of emergency, when we most need them.

It's Your Move. Make the Most of It.

In addition to being a canvas for idea collection, the Idea Zone can help you become the dream weaver for your next job opportunity. Like the world beyond the secret passage of the Narnia wardrobe door, you can test out your distinct talents in a world where anything is possible.

The agile careerist consistently iterates the ideas that answer the questions, "What do I want that I currently don't have in my life's work?" or "What do I want to do next?"

Knowing you have options is a fundamental step in figuring out what's next.

Agile thinking happens when an individual embraces the principles of responsive career navigation while flirting with the storage tank of concepts and ideas in motion. Winning the next fulfilling job, being happy in the current job, or planning for what's next is part of a continuum of iterative and parallel efforts.

Whether you work in a corporation or are an entrepreneur with your own business, your job is subject to change. A career is dynamic and will benefit from calibration and fresh infusions of new mental visions on a regular basis.

Action Figure or Pause Button

One of Sir Isaac Newton's laws of motion is a great metaphor for the two basic mindsets for modeling a career in a constantly changing landscape:

1. An object in motion tends to stay in motion.
2. An object at rest tends to stay at rest.

Let's take a look at these two groups.

The Interval/Rest Stop Risks Stagnation

A person with an interval mindset sees the current job as the goal. Based on a specific point of view, a considerable amount of energy and exploration are expended to acquire the true north job. A feeling of *I have arrived* takes over.

Truly successful people will tell you an achievement is a stepping stone, not a moment of arrival. Danger lurks among complacent attitudes in any work domain. A rest stop resulting from an interval mindset is analogous to viewing a workplace as a job, rather than an element of a fluid career.

A rest stop mimics a plateau instead of a progressive journey achieved by the hike up the mountain.

What happens when all the vigorous efforts used to attain the perfect job are derailed? What is your Plan B? This can happen when a bold career jump is not tested or explored in advance of a move. Landing a job out of alignment with who you are can feel more like a prison sentence than an opportunity for growth.

The Secrets of People in Motion and Their Idea Zone

Have you ever noticed that certain resilient people continually land on their nimble feet, regardless of the setbacks in their lives? Their careers are recession proof. Even when they lose a job, another one better suited to them magically appears.

People who enjoy movement have a magic formula. Just like the hiker who crosses the stream in an agile way, these motion-obsessed individuals make incremental changes to accommodate their personal preferences and undeniable dreams. They recognize the cadence of gradual change as a smart system of gratifying progress. The steady flow of forward movement provides a better view of what's next. And it is far preferable to the tornado effect of abrupt change caused by circumstances out of our control.

People in motion invent Plan B and beyond in the form of the Idea Zone.

When the external factors of uncertainty and change start to orbit around them, they take notice. When their internal interests evolve, they take notice. Self-awareness steers their career machine.

And finally, they take action. In the game of career navigation, big opportunities and progress are derived from small refinements over time. The prepared idea generator individual and long-term player are equipped to fine tune the unpredictable aspects of the zigzag journey.

Self-Awareness Game Day

Making career decisions feels a bit like playing *Jeopardy*. Choosing the right category of knowledge is the difference between an easy garden path of correct questions and the unexpected turmoil of negotiating a rocky incline. Depending on your self-awareness and where you are in your career journey, some categories are easier than others.

There are three categories of self-awareness and related questions:

1. Personal Brand and Preferences: Who am I? What am I good at? What do I like?

2. Career Path: What type of job do I want? What industry do I prefer? What role do I like? What's next?

3. Project and Job Performance: How can I perform well within my current job or project? How can I improve?

The next story is a great blend of all three categories, with a special emphasis on career path.

The Idea Force Awakens

She is an action figure.

When Amber Porter Telfer, a Gen Xer on the cusp of Gen Y, first shared her agile career story, I leaned forward, captivated by her words. Like a soccer player, Amber knows when to go all out and when to turn quickly and sharply to tame the moving ball, outwitting her opponent.

Her hearty laugh and dimpled smile complement her high-octane enthusiasm for work and life.

I first met Amber at a Startup Executive Roundtable dinner in late fall 2010, when the leaves had vanished and the winds were swirling in a menacing pattern in the Windy City. Unlike other networking events, the small group size enabled the five of us to fully share our stories and pose thoughtful questions.

Amber's story was the perfect icebreaker in the warm, soft lighting of Shaw's Crab House. She was a transplant from California to Chicago, a statement you don't hear very often in the land of relentless and icy winters. We discovered Amber spent seven years as an information systems analyst for the US Army during Operation Iraqi Freedom, working on communications systems. The members of this roundtable group wondered what it was like to be a woman in the military in a technology role.

Her response was, "I learned I am more capable than I thought." The guys who processed technology jobs alongside her liked to tinker with technology, translating into longer service times. "Me? I just got right down to business." Her boss remarked, "You fix more technology issues than anyone on the team."

Aside from being a significant confidence booster, her time in technology opened up considerable doors within multiple professions and industries. She was a VP of digital at a global communications agency when we met, but like the others at the table, she pondered whether she could make a more noteworthy and satisfying contribution elsewhere.

When the conversation turned to startup ideas, Amber must have had them stored in her coat pocket because she shared a number of software and app-based ideas in quick succession. She described them in detail, like a seasoned strategist making her mark in an important boardroom. At one point the roundtable organizer, Manish Mehta, said, "You have lots of ideas. What businesses are you going to start?"

As I walked away from the table that evening, Amber's unique ability to adapt and invent was evident in more than her words. She was an action figure—a mover in heart and spirit. I was confident her street smarts and quick wit would clear the way for her inventive ideas.

Amber's story began most humbly many years before.

True Grit

Amber's uncertain early family circumstances required resilient responses peppered with grit, regarding her life's work. She started working before she was ten. Idea generation coupled with problem-solving skills earned her the only stability she could secure in a dysfunctional single-parent household.

They were poor. Have you ever seen those trees in public places during the holidays? The paper ornaments on the tree contain an individual's age and boy/girl status. One year her family's names were on a Christmas tree, ensuring each member of her family one gift from a kind stranger. She was so grateful for this act of kindness, yet she needed more.

If Amber wanted a pair of jeans or sunglasses, her paycheck was required. Beyond conventional babysitting jobs, she cleaned construction sites by organizing two-by-four stacks and removing cement from windows with her mother. She experienced heavy lifting and manual labor, while other girls her age were slowly growing out of childhood.

Amber knew how to create and nurture new ideas as she mastered the art of parallel entrepreneurship as a child.

With an eye for fashion and value, she worked at garage sales helping customers acquire their hidden treasures. With her long, dark wavy hair, and her genuine, sparkling brown eyes, her confident manner resulted in impressive sales. She earned a 25 percent commission.

Like the black onyx ring she purchased for herself at one of the garage sales, Amber was fiercely determined to attain her precious goals in life. And she was going to do it with style.

By the time she was fifteen, she lived independently, affording rent through multiple revenue streams. Her mother remarried, yet Amber was intent on living life on her own terms. With impressive street smarts and focused perseverance, she balanced her own class-cutting defiant actions with studying books on human behavior in the library. Time well spent as she continued to traverse a series of job experiments. She worked as a lifeguard, a waitress, a vintage shop sales manager, and personal banker to support herself.

Like the always-full pot of gold at the end of the rainbow, Amber's Idea Zone is a continuous cycle of creative thought. Her stream of ideas answers the questions, "What's next for me?" and "What more can I learn?"

Building Blocks of Career Evolution

When times were tough, Amber's stepdad gave her some sage advice: take the good and leave the bad behind. She took this one step further as she developed her personal mantra of "Get on with it."

As a young adult, she studied art in college before joining the army. Heavy lifting once again became a theme in her life as she excelled and endured the stringent boot camp requirements for mental and physical fitness. As a proud army veteran, Amber fully absorbs the meaning of sacrifice.

Just as she chipped the cement off of the dirty windows at the construction site for a clearer view in her youth, she peered into her future when she retired from the military.

Her Idea Zone was operating in full force. Art training and a fascination with the dotcom era highlighted her opportunity to overlay her strong technology skills with marketing. She knew her instincts were correct when the ascent of digital marketing created abundant opportunities for dramatic career growth.

The Idea Explosion

Amber can best be described as a solo multipreneur—an individual who pursues multiple business activities as a portfolio, either serially or in parallel.

She is now an entrepreneur running four businesses in parallel: a flower farm in southern Michigan, a marketing consultancy, an online vintage clothing resale shop, and a photography studio in Chicago. All businesses rely on her brilliant sense of fashion and impeccable style. She uses her technology and marketing backgrounds to manage and grow her businesses. In her own words, Amber understands who she is: I like creating things that have not been done before.

Amber's prolific idea flow unlocked door number one, door number two, and door number three as she navigated the rugged terrain of job opportunities.

Yet real life and real careers collide on a regular basis. Careers are riddled with detours like toxic work environments and medical setbacks.

Amber's day-to-day life is not all hearts and flowers. She lives with a few medical challenges. The heavy lifting she did while in the military left its physical mark and led to a persistent amount of chronic pain. Through a few surgeries and a dedicated effort to physical therapy, she continues to move forward with an optimistic smile and a powerful drive. And lots of ideas.

Barriers and Roadblocks

Like Joseph Campbell's hero's journey—a character and story arc structure used by writers and storytellers to capture the reader's attention—there is a defining moment in the career journey. When this happens, the career warrior is overcome by the threat of sinister danger and ominous failure. Yes, your career path is subject to unwanted detours. This is precisely the moment when agility and fierce determination inhabit the character of the career hero.

Similar to Amber's response to challenges, it is essential to cultivate the ability to weave through the calamity and adapt to imperfect circumstances.

Next Steps

Idea generation and creativity are highly valued contributions in the workplace. Design thinking exercises are fast becoming one of the useful facilitation platforms for solving business problems. Companies that do not innovate will not grow, nor will they survive. The same holds true for individuals. Consider a few of the following exercises to sharpen your skills:

1. Create an Idea Zone with an Idea Tracker.

   - Track your ideas for one week. Capture all of your ideas in a notebook, a digital document, or wherever is most convenient. Keep them in one place.

   - Record your ideas without questioning them, early in the morning, late at night, during the day, after a walk, or after a workout. Like Drew, collect links, articles, and stories that interest you.

After one week, take a look at the types of ideas and organize them into categories:

- Personal Brand and Preferences: Who am I? What am I good at? What do I like?

- Career Path: What type of job do I want? What industry do I want? What role do I want? What's next?

- Project and Job Performance: How can I perform well with my current job or project? How can I improve?

2. When you have one of those difficult days at work, review your personal Idea Zone for five to ten minutes.

- Start to explore the possibilities. Do any of your ideas include hobbies or side interests? Do any of your ideas present solutions to your current project or people problem?

- How does it make you feel to think of other possibilities in your work or hobby?

- Review your list the following day. How do your feelings differ the next morning vs. how you felt during your difficult day? Note the power you have by focusing on positive ideas for your future.

3. Answer the question, "What do I do or read to stay current with business and industry trends?"

- Write down the blogs, articles, and books that influence your thinking about your industry and career into the Idea Zone.

- Create a list of key learnings from your reading list.

- When you attend a conference, create a list of ideas you gained from the conference.

CHAPTER 3

Principle Two: Pursue It in Parallel

The best place to invent the future is away from our desk.
—SIMON SINEK, BEST-SELLING LEADERSHIP
AUTHOR AND SPEAKER

Parallel Tracking

In this chapter, you will learn the value of moving beyond a single-track sequential career focus to pursuing activities in parallel. This nimble principle is a practical guide to multiple-track thinking, doing, and planning. In practice, it mimics a well-coached track team, rather than a three-ring circus.

Similar to the discipline of project management, the success of shrewd career navigation benefits from smart scheduling and real-time peripheral vision. Parallel pursuits require the finesse of accomplishing certain activities side by side, while distinguishing what must be done in sequential order.

The manufacturing industry illustrated the wisdom of simultaneous tasks by shortening time-to-market timetables. Concurrent scheduling and automation techniques revolutionized mass-production assembly lines, from cars to every form of electronics. The useful concept also compressed and increased efficiencies in complex long-term software development schedules.

Parallel pursuits fall into three types of side activities:

1. **Education**

   As in a busy galaxy, learning opportunities surround you and continue to explode with inventive instruction schemes. Examples include formal school studies, online training, conference education, and experiential learning while trying something new. The knowledge transfer comes from knowledge basics, skills acquisition, or theory analysis.

2. **Side Projects**

   Side interests come in two flavors: a hobby or a paying side gig.

   Hobby

   You approach hobbies or passions with authentic curiosity and interest. As a multidimensional being, you are more than your current line of work. We all have creative ideas about what we want to do in our "spare" time.

   A hobby may catch your eye, presenting you an ideal platform for growth and the cultivation of divergent thinking. Sample hobbies include taking up a craft like woodworking, learning about space exploration, or participating in an investment club with a group of novices.

Side Gig

The gig economy definition:

A labor market characterized by the prevalence of short-term contracts or freelance work, as opposed to permanent jobs

Also known as a side hustle, a side gig refers to working on the side in addition to a full- or part-time job. Some workers cobble together several side gigs as a work style, intentionally creating multiple revenue streams. They mix and match their talents with available assignments.

When working full time or part time at your main job, a side gig may compel you into action by enticing you with extra income. Bonus: you can test your burgeoning ancillary skills in the market.

3. **Role expansion**

Every profession requires a fundamental level of knowledge via do-it-yourself learning, apprenticeship experience, skills training, or formal education. Once basic skills are acquired and a desired role is attained, the incremental expansion of your role begins. Learning on the job and volunteering for increased responsibilities are examples of making your job bigger. The habit of role extension expands your professional stature while amplifying your value in industries like finance, social work, or the teaching profession.

Now, let's delve deeper into the design and construction of parallel activities guided by purpose and inspired exploration.

Career Architecture via Parallel Pursuits

Remember Lego bricks? Twice named "Toy of the Century," the bricks are the foundation elements of the Denmark-based global company. Childhood ideas and creative expression are hallmark features of the customer experience defined by play.

Launching a career starts with a sketchy blueprint created somewhere between childhood dreams and the education of young adults. Similar to the assembly of iconic Lego building bricks, we follow our plans for a time and rearrange them to form various configurations. Whether our decisions are formulated on a whim or due to long-term tedious planning, flexibility of building bricks is key to the success of our career system.

With a passion for the study of architecture, design, and technology careers, I analyzed a diverse assortment of frameworks. Applying these flexible concepts to career design and management resulted in a Career Architecture framework. The system allows for revisions timed with monthly, quarterly, or yearly self-directed reviews. Ingredients of the planning template include education, training, experience, and personal motivation. The building blocks accumulate with incremental job experiences and interests acquired throughout the career journey.

Using toy Lego bricks as an analogy to launch and nurture a career, multiple Lego creations take place in parallel. Examples are construction characters like Bionicles and superheroes, colorful brick masterpieces, robot design, and vehicle assembly.

In career evolution, parallel activities might converge to form one wholly fresh invention. Or, as the architect of these plans, a worker may change lanes to focus on a related aspect of the career journey. A lane change venture sparks the next stage of your iterative career.

CAREER ARCHITECTURE

SKILLS
STRENGTHS
INTERESTS

+

TRAINING
EDUCATION
HOBBIES

=

PORTFOLIO OF SKILLS
EXPERIENCE
KNOWLEDGE
INSIGHTS

ROLE 1   ROLE 2   ROLE 3

©Konstant
Change

Career architecture as a structured modular system relies on a combination of logical reason and versatility of additive elements. With the interlocking capability of Lego bricks, the career designer will level up or combine the parallel construction elements.

AGILE CAREERIST JOURNEY

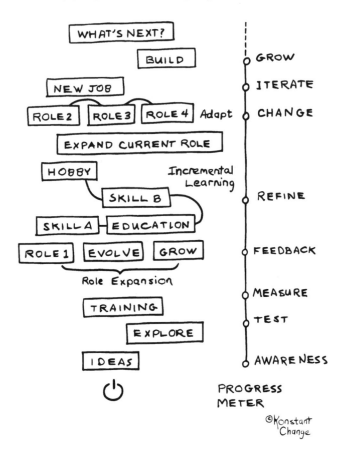

Many of the components spring from the parallel dimensions of:

- Education
- Side Projects
- Role Expansion

Let's explore the details of these dimensions.

Education

An essential strategy of the agile careerist is incremental accumulation of knowledge. A tactical weapon against the evaporating usefulness of a skill set, a dynamic education plan will fortify knowledge and keep pace with change.

A formal education, like an advanced degree or certificate program, will strengthen your expertise in a particular industry or provide structure for absorbing a new body of knowledge. Unless your employer is funding the program, this is the costliest education path.

Resourceful individuals with a passion for learning and a lean wallet, however, can design their own programs, like a virtual MBA or advanced training in financial services. Although not credentialed, the skills gained through online courses by universities, business schools, massive open online courses (MOOCs), Lynda.com (part of LinkedIn), Coursera, CreativeLive, and Udemy provide valuable content and training.

The best part? These options are low cost or no cost!

The explosion of reasonably priced online courses by individual thought leaders creates useful offerings via the rise of how-to solopreneurs. These creative entrepreneurs offer numerous choices for learning and exploration of new ideas.

We live in the middle of a knowledge Renaissance. YouTube videos and TED Talks are popular contributors to the information kingdom. All we have to do to claim intelligence riches is log in and learn.

Upskill to Stay Relevant

Skills update courses are another way to ensure personal relevance in the workplace. Ten-week courses offered by education companies like General Assembly enable workers to "skill up" in the areas of design, marketing, technology, and data. For example, an engineer or product manager may consider enhancing product management expertise or learning about agile methods to advance her career.

The skills education companies fill the knowledge gap left by outdated content and techniques learned during our baseline education jaunt.

Finance and medical professionals participate in numerous educational courses to stay current with trends and to advance in their roles. The medical profession, in particular, has built this philosophy into their continuing education requirements. After all, wouldn't you want a doctor performing your surgery to be knowledgeable about the latest developments?

Corporations, while slow to the party on customized internal learning opportunities, are starting to reconfigure their employee education systems. The push approach to structured on-the-job training is gradually being replaced by an employee self-directed approach to learning, all provided by the employer. With this method, employees choose their areas of interest, thus taking responsibility for their own career advancement, rather than relying on a one-size-fits-all for employee training.

Side Interests
Blue Sky Ideas and Hobbies
Think back to the "What if?" game when someone asks, "What would you do if you won the lottery?" Do you remember how you felt? Maybe you were wistful, maybe you were smiling. Your brain opened up unlimited possibilities. You likely answered the question with a greater sense of clarity regarding priorities than before the question was posed.

Hidden among the treasures of these immediate impressions are activities you might consider pursuing on the side.

How did you answer the question regarding the lottery scenario? Maybe you decided to dabble in a side business more captivating than your day job. Or thought about quitting your job to help solve a global problem like drinking water scarcity. The wanderlust urge may have beckoned you to travel the globe and refine your photography passion. Sometimes newfound time made possible by a lottery win might lead to the simple pleasures in life, like reading more books or learning a new craft.

Take a moment to review some of your answers. And start to ponder the aspirations that follow "What if?"

Los Angeles-based Ben Tseitlin, a web designer and writer, started making yummy healthy chocolates as a hobby. With no domain expertise in food design or preparation, he relied on curiosity and passion to master the specialty craft when he launched Benchic Chocolate. He now spreads the joy of creations made from high-quality natural ingredients through chocolate-making classes and kits.

The hobbies and activities driven by curiosity and genuine attraction to a topic without consideration of financial gain open the gates to the pursuit of happiness. The potpourri of side interest options include:

- Join a nonprofit board with a cause that resonates with you

- Take a creative class like dance, theater, or art to explore a different side of you

- Join a club, like a book club, a running club, or extreme sports club

- Start a new hobby you thought was only possible with the lottery scenario
- Participate in meetups with topics that interest you, not related to your profession
- Get involved in an association within your industry or a new industry
- Volunteer to participate as a youth sports coach
- Sign up for industry networking events and get involved
- Attend events and lectures outside of your industry
- Sign up for a personal development online experience
- Join a dinner club
- Start a small group of your own, if what you are looking for does not exist

Exploring new areas of interest outside your main professional focus opens up neural pathways in brain development. The process of studying science or math, if they are outside your area of expertise, will contribute to unique perspectives for defining and solving problems.

Remember Drew Marshall from Chapter 2, where we explored the Idea Zone principle?

He is the voracious idea collector who squirreled away his observations and insights in a readily accessible storage tank in his brain. He kept his ideas alive by capturing them in a notebook, elaborating on the concepts with others, and turning inklings into fully developed thoughts.

Learning new things by exploring topics from your Idea Zone

activates the needle in your happiness meter. Giving yourself permission to daydream, on occasion, will generate hope and well-being during challenging times.

Pursuing side interests frequently has the gratifying effect of blossoming into paid side jobs or breaking fertile ground for an alternate career.

Side Gigs and Freelance Assignments

Working on the side translates into extra income—particularly useful when your personal life requires extra tuition payments for your children or there are unexpected living expenses. Or you may be saving up for the trip of a lifetime.

Freelance or consulting assignments are examples. Your side gig may be an extension of your current role. For example, if you shoot video and write scripts at an advertising agency, you can generate side income by producing video and editing work for your own clients.

Platforms like Upwork, Artisan, or DesignCrowd enable you to provide skills like design services, application/web development, or technical writing. Many industries have launched online platforms in areas like counseling, therapy, telemedicine, and career coaching.

According to the Institute for the Future (IFTF), which has studied the future of work for fifty years, the on-demand economy includes tens of millions of people already making their living on platforms. They state: online platforms not only have the ability to benefit both clients and providers, they also show immense potential to better address issues like underemployment and skill development. A study by McKinsey suggests that over 540 million people will benefit from online platforms.

Role Expansion

Similar to the first Lego brick required for bringing projects to life, an entry-level position interlocks with incremental roles to expand the cumulative career.

Role expansion in career development is comparable to product and service expansion strategies in corporations. With an add-on system mentality, the Lego Group expanded from bricks, to characters, to robots, to vehicles, to superheroes.

Jeannie Walters expanded from the role of web-based marketing services to customer experience investigation™. She expanded her expertise into a role that helps corporations make better decisions regarding marketing and corporate strategy.

For twelve years, she helped large corporations bring their companies online in the form of websites and online marketing activities. As a partner in a productive thirty-five-person firm, her moment of reckoning happened when the firm won a significant contract for an insurance company. The project to create and implement a quoting and processing system felt more like an information technology program.

She was truly grateful for this important work, yet observed, "This is not marketing anymore." She identified market research and defining customer needs as critical components of any successful product or service. Jeannie wanted to make better use of her listening skills, empathy, and talent for communication.

Jeannie noticed a communication gap between companies and their clients. She wondered who advocated for the customer and what human experiences and feedback were missing from the research, product development, and customer satisfaction equations. She started a company to care for the customer point of view.

Her unique customer experience investigation process helps businesses design and deliver positive experiences and products worthy of customer interest and loyalty. Through market and individual insights, Jeannie's company, 360Connext, helps companies monitor trends, streamline product offerings, and retain customers.

She expanded her role into Chief Customer Experience Investigator™ by creating a hybrid role at the intersection points of research, strategy, marketing, and the greater good.

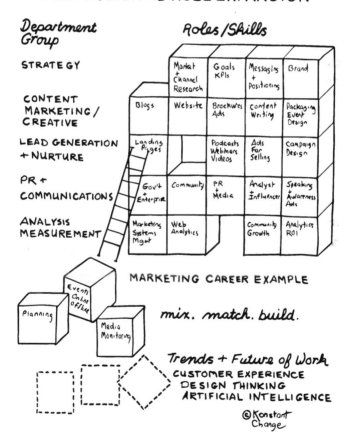

PROFESSIONAL ROLE EXPANSION

Pick One. It's Your Move.

What does role expansion look like in a specific profession?

The building block diagram on the previous page illustrates myriad entry points for a profession such as marketing. The novice worker starts with one or two areas in the multiple-choice grid. He may start as a writer for promotional copy for lead generation tactics and branch into media relations as a next step. The game of mix and match provides plentiful possibilities.

A marketing careerist may spend her entire career within these building elements or jump out of the marketing grid into a related complementary product management grid.

Questions like "What area of the business interests me?" and "What specialty will make me more valuable?" beg for attention in the universe of fine-tuning and tweaking for best fit.

Parallel Pursuits: The Ultimate Power Play

Nimble management of parallel pursuits is a power play in the work sphere for balancing uncertainty with certainty. The smart move of preserving your main job pays your monthly bills. Feeding your passion in a nonpaying hobby or side interest enables you to explore freely while developing your talents or improving your skills.

Order from Chaos

With art and mathematics as my blended muse, I found the idea of parallel lines in high school geometry to be an elegant structure for order in a chaotic world. The lines could span infinity or have specific start and end points.

In doodling fashion I embraced the activity of drawing lines that intersected the parallel lines. Drawing multiple intersecting lines resulted in the creation of geometric shapes. As in your life's work, the intersection points formed by angled or perpendicular lines erupt with activity and possibilities of the unknown.

Fully immersed in the world of computer systems and technology marketing, I witnessed the evolution of parallel processing on desktop computers. At one time, software tasks were accomplished sequentially. This was a time-consuming and frustrating way to get through the workday. Now, applications and processes work in parallel, forming a reliable multiplier for triumphant productivity. Data can be processed concurrently on multiple processors. Yay!

Like the vision of parallel universes with numerous outcomes, more can be accomplished on multiple tracks than on a single track.

Using the logic of math and flexibility of the creative intellect, I maneuvered through my agile career path, full of parallel paths and glorious intersecting points.

Adventures in Parallel Pursuits

The idea of expanding a workday beyond the perimeter of already overextended lives can be a daunting proposition. Yet the time invested does not have to be onerous or overwhelming.

Many individuals who explore side pursuits become more organized and make room for serendipity, the gateway to unexpected discoveries. The act of uncovering a latent passion or making extra income infuses people with remarkable energy. Similar to fostering idea collection in The Idea Zone, creative pursuits stimulate positive thoughts and contribute to a sense of control.

And like insurance coverage, a backup plan will cover you when the unforeseen circumstances catapult you into the universe of uncertainty. Establish a "No worries. I've got this." frame of mind, a useful attitude on the career obstacle course.

Boot Camp for Parallel Practice: My Experiment

The Dream

The visualization of my first graphic design job, however unrealistic in the expectations realm, included promotion and marketing of clever tech products in a contemporary communications department. In my fairytale vision, designers, photographers, illustrators, and copywriters collaborated in dynamic teams. We were surrounded by colorful, inspirational artwork on the walls, abundant creative tools, and technology.

In the dream, we would hash out stellar ideas in conference rooms while the sun shone in the late afternoon, illuminating our killer concepts. As we laughed and sometimes debated contrasting points of view, our department would earn a reputation as a creative center of excellence.

The Reality

In reality, my first professional experience as a graphic designer in a male-dominated telecommunications company was more like a stranger in a strange land. With a nod to the highly heralded science fiction book, Robert Heinlein's *Stranger in a Strange Land*, it took me some time to grok the ways of technology companies.

Engineers who marched to the vision of the founder were lauded as leaders of excellence. There were no awards for the creative department. The sun never streamed into the windowless meeting rooms. Graphic designers were at the bottom of the food chain of noticeable contribution.

Once my dreams melted into reality, I wisely assimilated into the pulse of work in a telecommunications infrastructure company. I confidently absorbed the duties of my graphic design role, among the prickly thorns of my male colleagues within a hard-charging department and industry.

Thrown into the wild frontier of locker room antics and strong-willed temperaments among my coworkers, I developed a thick skin. The adaptable mindset was part of my survival kit to navigate the random crass behavior.

My proudest role was technology translator and technology lingo interpreter. I deciphered complex technical concepts, turning them into simple diagrams, photos, and content. My practical communication skills helped customers and interested buyers understand and purchase networking equipment.

The building dress code offered an opportunity to adopt an integral aspect of the technology culture while earning my place as one of the guys on the team. With our department digs adjacent to the manufacturing facility door, I conformed to the style of my coworkers. My fashion statement included hooded sweatshirts, casual blouses, t-shirts, Levi's jeans, and corduroys.

Despite ignoring the Dress for Success code defined in non-technology industries, I expanded my initial design role to include the roles of art director, package designer, and commercial product photographer. At times, I was overwhelmed by the long hours and rough-and-tumble environment, yet hung in there for the experience. My first exposure to balancing multiple jobs and acquiring new skills set a high bar for subsequent ventures.

All the while, I clearly visualized running my own creative agency business for technology enterprises. I had barely scratched the surface of developing the necessary skills for my profession. There was so much more to learn on the road to mastering my craft.

The overconfidence of youth is stunning.

The Parallel Pursuits

With access to the tools of advertising and marketing departments, I quickly realized I could take on freelance gigs. This accomplished two things: experience with marketing products beyond networking equipment and the enticing reward of extra income.

Although my personal business network was small, the ground was fertile for new business. My unintended competitive low-pricing model, based on minimal fixed costs, attracted an impressive roster of new clients.

One of the commercial printers in the region served as a conduit for new customers, helping me discover the value of acquiring business through channels. I started a lead-sharing group in our business community to build and nurture relationships. A business acquaintance hired me to create a catalogue for his manufacturing business.

Firmly establishing myself in the vital roles of sales and business development, I learned ventures live and die with the sales function. Beyond the "better, cheaper, or faster" mandate for launching a new company, building relationships is a required effort of any business owner.

The evening and weekend endeavors flourished into the desired status of entrepreneur.

Within three years, I generated enough business to launch a marketing communications firm. My side gig morphed into a newly formed corporation. Within one year, I merged my business with another local designer. We were the only female-owned communications enterprise focusing on tech companies in the western technology corridor of Chicago.

Foray into the Future

The evergreen lessons harnessed by moving from the curiosity question of "What if?" to the risk-taking actions of starting something new emerge into stories of grit. When the side gig mentality surfaces, the inevitable urge to jump in without overthinking ignites an unstoppable momentum.

The future of work assures a divergent path brimming with multiple-choice options. While essays in a testing environment measure knowledge retention as an accurate reflection of what we already know, the blank page of your future can cause anxious tremors. The essay test on the jungle trek through our so-called career of life should be based on aspirations and glorious intentions written in future tense, not past tense.

The side hustle emerged as a sensible way to diversify income and to explore what-ifs for passion discovery. Passions arise from experiences, unlike pearls uncovered in a journey of self-discovery. A side gig unlocks a playground for creative experimentation and accumulation of valued skills on the quest to unveil passions.

Much has been written about the financial upside of the side hustle, yet pursuing jobs and interests on the side also develops an impressive portfolio of case studies. Success in the side hustle establishes credibility in the categories of big shoulders and juggling management.

According to researchers, a job as a pragmatic tool for income generation evolves with careerists who demand satisfaction and meaning as part of the equation. Side hustles offer a bridge to meet the great expectations of our time.

The Half-Life of Learned Skills

The methodical accumulation and creative application of knowledge are reasonable responses by agile careerists who embrace learning as a lifelong journey. Education is a launching pad, rather than a key, to the ideal line of work.

Baseline education is in danger of becoming outdated much more quickly than in past decades. A technology innovator like Tesla's Elon Musk demonstrates the need for advanced learning systems as he disrupts the status quo, bypassing the boundaries of present-day knowledge. Disruptive technologies like Tesla's automotive designs and SpaceX's advanced rockets depend on knowledge outside the scope of available university curriculums.

The strongest driver for treating education as a starting point, with steady incremental upgrades to your profession, is the dwindling half-life of learned skills. Originally coined for chemistry and physics, the definition of half-life is: the time it takes for something to degrade to half its original value.

Salim Ismail, a Silicon Valley author of *Exponential Organizations*, investor, entrepreneur, and recent executive director of Singularity University, assesses the half-life of knowledge has moved from thirty years to five years in the span of one generation. Fully immersed in exponential technologies and organizations, he believes education systems must evolve to accommodate steady advancements. As global ambassador at Singularity, he helps individuals, businesses, institutions, investors, NGOs, and governments understand and utilize technology to positively impact billions of people.

"Learning decay" insights create a compelling justification for commitment to lifelong learning. College degrees construct a baseline for startup careerists. Like software updates frequently delivered to our devices, individuals will benefit from updates to their personal learning systems.

Job titles and occupations are floating off the relevance scale. The ascent of artificial intelligence is another chapter of creative destruction, where certain skills are demolished and others rise from the ashes. The promised land of career abundance lies in the job descriptions not yet invented.

Multiskilled workers who complement machine intelligence will win the relevance challenge in the coming years. Side gigs and Plan B career exploration present abundant potential for astute career strategists.

The world of work is changing. Professionals who do not evolve will not survive. Their personal operating systems will crash and burn.

The Magic of Self-Direction

Employees are in charge of their work experiences and accountable for the progression of their careers.

Just as cars require consistent maintenance and automotive systems need to be balanced and aligned, people also require timely updates and tune-ups. When people are out of alignment or short on brainpower, the foggy lines of confusion move in like hovering storm clouds.

Incremental education in the form of curated learning experiences is a viable parallel pursuit ensuring future career relevance.

It has never been easier to systematically recalibrate skills or satiate hunger for side interests and hobbies. No-cost education in the form of MOOCs and low-cost online training through Coursera or Udemy are readily available. Certificate coursework and single refresher classes are accessible for a variety of professions like finance, engineering, and marketing.

If a corporation's training systems do not include this type of education for its employees, the agile careerist will design her own curated programs to future-proof her career. The well-trained individual with current skills will forge his way to the promotion path. Meanwhile, the half-life calculation sounds the warning bell of declining skills and potential job loss.

Now that we've reviewed the various types of side endeavors, let's explore a real-life example of someone who turned "What if?" into "Why not?" Let's see how parallel thinking can be applied to the contemporary career navigator.

Hackathon Decoder in a Bow Tie

When I launched a marketing hackathon event at a tech incubator, it attracted an eclectic group of entrepreneurs, business strategists, and marketers. Like group therapy for problem solvers, individuals bonded over shared challenges and animated deliberation of viable solutions in structured exercises.

Ryan Rasmussen, the chestnut-haired young man with the direct, earnest gaze, readily facilitated one of the mastermind exchanges. Sporting a bow tie and hip oxfords, he looked like the creative agency artist types I often hired to launch technology software products.

With his signature "drive-by consulting" style, Ryan posed the probing questions necessary to gather insights and stimulate beneficial dialogue. Behaving like a seasoned consultant, his super listening powers paved the way for properly defining the problem before starting the debate.

The success of the hackathon was dependent on committed catalysts like Ryan. What I discovered throughout the weekend was Ryan's "helper of humans" nature.

Basic Training for an Extraordinary Journey

Ryan, a member of the initial wave of the millennial generation, is a curiosity wizard, a foundation character trait of the agile careerist.

During elementary school, Ryan was impatient in an academic environment. He finished tests early and was bored sitting in his seat. He did not know how to challenge ideas and conventional thinking during those formative years, but he created a storehouse of thoughts and questions for future reference.

Before Ryan ventured down the artist path in college, he admired the brilliant creative work of Jim Henson. He dreamed of becoming the next artistic genius with far-reaching influence in the realm of popular culture. Ryan expressed, "I want to create and inspire."

Ryan's curiosity navigation system was a beacon for traveling beyond the predictable path forged from a college credential. With a degree in art, Ryan concluded he would secure an entry-level business job and shape the role into a custom fit for his talents.

The role-shaping strategy was befitting an artist. In an age of personalization, why not custom build the part of our lives that accounts for 40 percent of our waking hours?

Ryan viewed his college studies as basic training. He remarked, "Figure out your skill sets and how you think, and then apply it to your situation." Demonstrating wise accountability for his life's work, he used the wizarding wand of intention for career design.

Parallel Dimensions Over Time

Ryan's career testing ground started in retail store management for a company offering high-end specialty products. The most notable product was a do-it-yourself business planner. Sounds simple, right? A bit of customer service sprinkled with financial tracking and a dash of store management may have summed up his tenure at this popular retailer.

Yet Ryan transformed his starter position into an idea-generating annuity with future job dividends. His constant flow of questions and quick ability to implement ideas kicked off an evolutionary pattern in his job progression.

With his Harry Potter likability and daily fashionable suits, he created a memorable impression on the store floor. When asked about the genesis of his career in retail, he quipped modestly, "I built a new program. My education did not prepare me for this. As a nerd in retail, I adopted a few artistic tendencies and moved up."

Over the next few years, Ryan engaged in three parallel pursuits: retail store management, online media management, and product development. Like the Ironman competition, where triathletes train in parallel for the events of swimming, bicycling, and running, Ryan balanced multiple disciplines. He soared beyond job titles, often creating new job descriptions.

The First Parallel

In 1999, three authors, Christopher Locke, Doc Searls, and David Weinberger, published a series of theses on the web known as *The Cluetrain Manifesto*, examining the impact of the internet on marketing strategies and tactics. They suggested conventional marketing techniques would need to evolve to online conversations to be understood by consumers and companies. These provocative theses were published in a book in 2000.

In his first parallel pursuit, with *The Cluetrain Manifesto* as his inspiration, Ryan pursued online conversations as a new way to promote products and enhance customer service. He launched an innovative blog, attracting a diverse blend of readers and potential customers. He established a blogger outreach program with devoted bloggers who loved the company's distinctive high quality notebooks, leather products, and personal workplace accessories.

His conversation strategy intersected directly with people, rather than a typical mass communication approach. Participating in a book called *The Age of Conversations*, he shared his insights about the rising influence of communication between customers and prospective buyers of popular brands.

Without a blueprint, Ryan built a community and established a digital presence. This happened precisely at the same time the volcano called social media erupted.

Just as the farmer prepares the rich soil for the ambitious sprouts of spring, Ryan's inquisitive nature and creativity nurtured ample choices at every career crossroads.

Taming the Cyber Frontier with Analytics
The Second Parallel

Ryan's second parallel endeavor leveraged his knowledge of customer behavioral insights. As a vice president of research and analytics, he noticed the cavernous void of social analytics tools. He pursued a side project developing measurement tools.

As the master architect for a suite of online and offline measurement tools, he created three products: Recommendation Index, Earned Digital Engagements, and Digital Footprint Index. He received awards from Harvard and Stanford, including a couple for Measurement Innovation and Product of the Year.

Batman by Night, Problem Solver by Day

Side gigs come in varying shades of financial necessity and pure quests for knowledge. Ryan's inquisitive approach to strengthening his business acumen and sincere desire to help others manifested an alter ego capable of ambitious accomplishments.

Journey to the Third Parallel

When I posed the question to Ryan, "What are you most proud of in your career?" he responded, "Think of me as Batman. By day I help companies solve problems, and by night I help entrepreneurs with problems ranging from finance to business strategy." At meetups, Ryan offers his knowledge insights to colleagues in need. Another side interest!

His caped crusade of knowledge transfer was refueled and energized when by night he worked toward his MBA.

He now works as a consultant for a marketing technology monitoring provider. Like a business mixologist, he swirls together a combination of technology, ideas, and rare listening skills.

Custom Fit

Ryan's ambitious juggling act is a rigorous example of working in parallel. Yet experimenting with this principle can be more like putting your toe in the water at the beach, rather than diving straight into the waves.

A career journey is different for each of us. The process of cultivating our unique dreams and taking small steps to achieve them will build the momentum necessary to move forward or make a lane change.

Consider other examples from this chapter:

- Jeannie Walters expanded her role from marketing services to Customer Experience Investigator™, building on her savvy marketing skills.

- Ben Tseitlin mastered the art of chocolate making on the side until he expanded it into a bigger business of helping others make chocolate creations.

- Freelance design services while working a corporate tech job turned into founding a technology marketing communications firm for me.

Next Steps

There are three different ways to explore the possibility of integrating a parallel pursuit into your life:

- Education
- Side Projects
- Role Expansion

Parallel pursuits fortify knowledge while making deposits into the employee value equation. Side gigs can expand choices and create lovely detours to meaningful work.

Pick one tactic from the current list:

1. Define job descriptions for your profession, including lateral skills acquisition and promotion paths. Create a role expansion building block diagram for your area of interest. If you are interested in a specific job function, schedule a phone call or coffee with someone who has the role to better understand the work experience. At the end of ninety days, what two or three options or combinations are you most attracted to?

2. Is there an achievable role expansion strategy available to you at your place of work? Does it require a credential? Make a list of options and start the exploration process of what it will take to expand your current role into the next position.

3. Make a list of potential side interests. Refine the list. Pick one side interest and pursue it for the sheer joy of learning something new.

4. Research a topic related to your career. Learn something new about your profession by taking an online tutorial or signing up for a course.

5. Jump into a side hustle by pursuing a paid freelance assignment separate from your current job. Create a summary of what you learned about yourself and your profession.

CHAPTER 4

Principle Three: A/B Test Your Career

Your experiences lead to passions.
— TINA SEELIG, BEST-SELLING AUTHOR AND
PROFESSOR, STANFORD UNIVERSITY

Tune Up Your Alternator

There is an Agile Marketing expression by Jascha Kaykas-Wolff, a leading technology marketer: don't be afraid to fail, but don't fail the same way twice. The point is to encourage risk and creativity, but learn from your mistakes. This sage advice regarding alternating between experience and test cycles applies to the agile career in the form of A/B tests.

Building on the principle of parallel pursuits from the last chapter, where we explored interests on the side, this chapter will cover testing your personal preferences for specific roles. The effective habit, referred to as the A/B Test Principle, is a matter of choice and an acknowledgement of success and failure. Do you choose Job A or do you choose Job B? Was Job A more successful or more a failure than Job B? Do you prefer the last job you had, or the one you have now?

Have your eyes ever been tested by an optometrist? The questions we hear are, "Which is better? Do you prefer this view, or is the next view better?" Similar to the vision test, where it feels like a clarity game, your point of view on job preferences depends on your singular set of optics.

This chapter will profile A/B testers in our midst and describe how to apply the A/B test. We will examine ways to monitor and learn from your work experiences within a fluid work environment. My goal in this chapter is also to shine a light on your instincts about your well-being, an integrated summary of your creativity, growth, and happiness.

The Test: Experience Over Instinct

At the start of your career, it's impossible to fully imagine the course of your career path until you have sampled a few things. The pressure to choose wisely by recent graduates can be ill placed, as the perfect job does not exist prior to a track record of experiences.

A/B Testing

The concept of A/B testing gives you permission to compare experiences with the wise intention of choosing the most advantageous endeavor for your talents. As a new college graduate or a mid-career professional, the modular flexibility of agile career architecture rules in favor of movement, rather than a standstill of frustration.

Agile career architecture, described in the last chapter, summarizes each job experience, framing out your roles, likes, dislikes, and expansion into new areas. It is a series of building block descriptions demonstrating progress and gathering the essential ingredients for your story.

Before you make a move, however, make sure you understand what you like and what you dislike about each of your work situations. Decipher your particular strengths and weaknesses. This type of self-awareness will enable you to more clearly recognize the better-fitting roles and look ahead to relevant job descriptions. Your ability to predict future success stories will improve as you measure your levels of creativity, growth, and happiness.

The Game of Choice

The test is simple. After you experienced more than one role, either concurrently or in sequence:

    A. Do you prefer Job A?

    B. Is Job B better?

    C. Or . . . do you like Job C better?

The test is scalable through many letters of the alphabet! Another perspective:

    A. Do you prefer your current position?

    B. Or is your side gig better?

Open-ended questions:

- How did breakthroughs from the setbacks and failures of Job A and Job B influence your job choice and work strategy in Job C?

- What were your successes in Job A and Job B? How would you describe what you liked about Job A and Job B?

- What did you dislike about Job A and Job B?

A/B TEST: GAME OF CHOICE

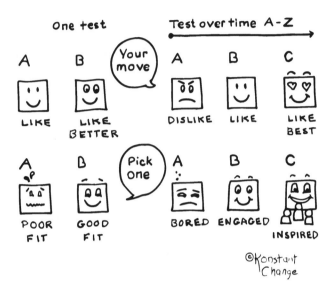

Each job addition sets up a competition between the previous, current, or concurrent roles. The winner or current role stays in play until you are drawn back to a similar role as before or advance to the next growth stage, setting up another test. As you build upon your agile career architecture system, you have the flexibility to move in any direction.

Have you ever considered the purchase of a house or a big-ticket item where it was difficult to make a decision? These types of decisions benefit from a comparative chart enabling you to rate your options. *Consumer Reports* reviews are a good example of a decision support tool, helping you to measure a product's features. The helpful report offers a checklist of characteristics and benefits, rating them on a comparative scale.

As a decision-making tool for career choice, it is useful to create your own report, measuring your satisfaction with sensible criteria:

- Create two or three columns, depending on how many jobs are in the comparison chute. The rows on the side include the filters of creativity, growth, and happiness included in the definition of the agile career:

  An agile career is a self-reflective, iterative career path guided by response to change, evolving job roles, and designed to optimize creativity, growth, and happiness.

- Beneath each column, rate these three characteristics with a numeric value.

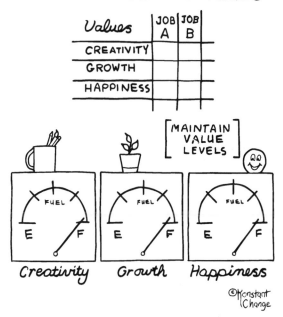

A historical view of job roles provides a clear snapshot of the strengths and weaknesses of each work position. When any of these aspects of work life are out of balance, the numbers in the columns decrease. Higher column totals are favorable. The three essential filters of creativity, growth, and happiness applied to each role enable you to build your unique career map while helping you make informed choices regarding the next job.

Experiences Lead to Passions

Experiences are at the origin of passion creation. Of the people interviewed for the Agile Careerist Project, 78 percent said their first job after training or formal education was the first job offer they received. Many first jobs are "good enough" roles, rather than ideal jobs. Some entry-level jobs deviate from the discipline they studied.

Imagination Meets Reality: A Sample A/B Test

Carmen Hill imagined her future but still made adjustments when faced with the confluence of unrestrained hope and workable reality. Since the age of nine, she was smitten with the idea of being a reporter. With a degree in journalism and broadcast news, she envisioned the life of TV personality Mary Tyler Moore in the city newsroom. She focused on the image of Mary boldly throwing her hat in the air on a Minneapolis downtown street. Confidence and happiness would accompany her on the streets and in the newsroom. She contemplated the gravity of news reporting, inspired by the search for truth in *All the President's Men.*

Her idol was Nellie Bly, a pioneer in investigative journalism. Carmen's idealist nature hungered to shine a light into dark places, making the world a better place with her questions and stories.

For a few years, Carmen manifested her personal storyline as a TV news reporter and producer. With the horizon making way for the technology tornado of the internet, she realized the game of workplace relevance transcended the dream job path. The pay was low, with fewer jobs in TV news than in fast-growing internet businesses. She clicked the reset button and launched an A/B test. Carmen eagerly rode into the technology frontier, expanding her opportunities rather than narrowing her options within broadcast news.

Carmen's A/B Test

Job A: Great job. Steep learning curve. Learned a lot. Not many advancement opportunities. Low pay. High on happiness and creativity scales. Low growth potential. Time to consider change.

Job B: As a potential industry, digital marketing had strong growth potential due to the explosion of the internet. Copywriting work leveraged skills from TV news.

Moving through the roles of copywriter, content strategist, digital marketer, and director of marketing for a digital customer experience agency, her soul-searching thirst for optimal job roles is ongoing. She shattered her original assumptions regarding broadcast news and A/B tested each new experience against past roles.

Awareness regarding strengths and weaknesses helped her to channel efforts in more optimal directions. Cataloguing failures and successes in the area of fit and projects added to her career architecture story. She now directs marketing for an agency, expanding her marketing role into the burgeoning discipline of digital experience.

Carmen effectively reset her focus each time, building upon accumulated skills and interests. She consistently studies the market to gauge growth potential. She ascends the stairway of career growth by acquiring knowledge and riding the waves of trends.

How Do You Know?

"You won't know until you try."

My first recollection of the question "How do you know?" happened at the age of five, when I refused to try something new at the dinner table. The strange-looking flat pizza dish looked like a sloppy concoction of leftovers topped with cheese. The collection of preferred tastes and the joy of testing a new dish require a couple behaviors: overcoming fear of the unknown and a desire to uncover a delectable taste sensation.

Observing the glee of my older siblings as they devoured the dinner, I taste-tested a small section of one slice and became a pizza convert. Yum!

My taste buds and palate were delighted when the messy heap of cheese, red sauce, and sausage of homemade pizza showed up on the dinner rotation. Pizza shot to the top of the list, in spite of my judgmental visual first impression of the food chaos. It's hard to believe there was a time when now-favorite meals were classified as unknown or untested.

Today, as a passionate purveyor of food creations, I thoroughly welcome adventures in cooking and cuisine. Through years of deliberate and sometimes unnerving experiments, my selection of preferred tastes has grown, giving me plentiful reasons to come back to the table.

As important as defining food preferences, I discovered the helpful feedback of failures. I swiftly delete those options from my diet.

The power of my mother's words, "You won't know until you try," resonates across life's moments of decision and indecision.

The power to choose, like the blessings of free will, comes with a responsibility to take the steps necessary to shape our useful inventory of likes and dislikes. No one but you is qualified to test the waters of multiple options or make a decision on the Goldilocks choice of what feels just right.

Testing One, Two, Three

Speaking of life's moments of choice, do you remember when you participated in your first sport? Childhood sports selection makes for an enlightening right of passage through the testing grounds of talents and failures.

Some of you may have spectacular memories of testing your abilities in baseball, softball, soccer, hockey, swimming, running, or volleyball. You know who you are because your natural hand-eye coordination and nimble moves stood out on the field. For others, the investigation of our talents in the sports arena may have resulted in a few angst-filled experiences before the integration of skills and confidence emerged.

Throughout the formative years of scrutinizing physical and mental abilities, questions like "What do I want?" "Is this right for me?" or "What do I like?" pepper the mind chatter within our daily routines.

When I was in grade school, slow-pitch sixteen-inch softball was quite popular in my neighborhood. I tried it and did not have much success. The pitch of a heavy hunk of leather hurled at my face caused me to swing too soon, too late, too high, or too low. The life strategy metaphor about keeping my eye on the ball mocked me. I was not a natural and did not smack the ball routinely enough to run around the bases very often. At least I made the effort to try the sport and in so doing stumbled upon my aptitude for speed and agility with other sports.

Alternative sports or activities like running, racquetball, swimming, and volleyball opened up avenues for genuine enjoyment and a lifetime flair for fitness. I redeemed myself by keeping my eye on the ball in activities outside the bases of the softball field. Similar to my lifelong food-tasting regimen, it was necessary to test my abilities across available athletic pursuits.

Running and hiking are my go-to choices for exercise today. My expanding reservoir of sports-related growth analogies include:

- Start by putting one foot in front of the other.
- Life is a marathon, not a sprint.
- It never gets easier. You just get stronger.

Mobile Global Citizen

In the fall of 2015, I met with Susan Oh in a New York café when I interviewed her for this book. We connected a few years prior when she lived in Chicago. She walked into the restaurant, her silky dark hair pulled back into a jazzy combination bun and ponytail, a few strands at each side of her face.

Dressed in an olive green t-shirt, off the shoulder on one side, and black pants, her chic appearance reminded me how New Yorker attitudes are expressed in fashion. New Yorkers have an astonishing ability to balance a casual image with a glimpse of sophisticated detail. They do this at every stylish turn, the way Italian women rock the trends with their museum-quality shoe artistry.

The Rise to Agility

Susan's life sounds like a lyrical composition filled with a search for meaning, cultivated by the observations of a precocious mind. She was born in a country of military rule in South

Korea, finding herself a few years later in Isfahan, Iran, where here father worked in petroleum until the Islamic Revolution. They fled the confusion in search of a safer environment.

The family found firmer footing in Calgary, Alberta, Canada, a mysterious flat land known as the "Texas of Canada" for its oil economy. To a young girl with no command of the English language, this was indeed a peculiar place. Susan remembered, "They thought we were weird and wondered if Korea was in Japan. They said, 'You look Chinese.'" Sigh.

Absorbing English as a second language, she found community and confidence in her voice and newly assimilated culture. In junior high school, she became proficient in French, another notch in the value scale for human relevance and communication.

The Art of Creating a Niche

Using convenience stores as her work lab, Susan learned to program registers, supporting the family business with technology acumen. She bused tables at local restaurants. She developed a full immersion training attitude.

In her formative years, Susan cultivated a strong-willed sense of independence. Although she was not an athlete, she attended a high school designed for Canadian Olympians because she was drawn to the flexible schedules. She decided to work as a journalist and crafted a strategy for becoming a writer. She wanted to explore the world and at times imagined reporting in a warzone.

Setting Up the Test with Job A

At the age of sixteen, she landed a role with the Canadian Broadcasting Company for the 1988 Olympics in Seoul, South Korea. Her multilingual skills secured her a seat among the journalists covering the Olympics. She rode the bus with them, wrote stories, and built her network.

When the Olympics concluded, Susan had just completed her first professional career test as a sports journalist. Her baseline professional experience started a role comparison platform to compare future writing jobs.

Expand the Boundaries of a Profession

Flanked by a degree in journalism and a minor in political science, Susan's attraction to the global stage led her to Hong Kong. She furthered her job skills during an internship in print journalism, working for a premier English newspaper at the business desk.

While in Hong Kong over the next four years, Susan expanded her writing capabilities beyond print into live broadcast news for CNBC Asia and then back into print for publications like *Newsweek*. She helped produce and write for two primetime shows for CNBC, building processes from scratch. While supporting production of these shows, Susan ritually worked fifteen-hour days. The economic pulse of the times required swift decisions as property values jumped 30 percent overnight and the thirst for news in Asia became insatiable.

In the spirit of A/B testing roles during this time, she performed as a news associate, producer, section editor, travel correspondent, and reporter. Working directly for the outlets or in a freelance capacity, she extended her subject matter competence in the areas of financial investments, business ethics, travel, pop culture, and entertainment.

Susan's A/B Test Examples
Job A: Sports journalist for the Olympics. Made connections. Learned the business. Wanted to learn more about

journalism opportunities and finish school. Focus on growth and continued learning.

Job B: Business print journalism at the news desk in Hong Kong. Viewed as stepping stone for print and business beat. More focus on growth. Time to set up a new test.

Next Test

Job A: CNBC Asia live broadcast news. Worked as producer for eighteen hours of live programming. Steep learning curve and long hours. High on creativity and growth; happiness in question due to escalating burnout. Preference for print journalism. Make a change.

Job B: Back in print, reporter for publications like *Newsweek*. Wanted to build out areas like travel and entertainment. Make a change by covering additional industries and publications.

The A/B tests continued from there.

Teasing out the possibilities inside the writing profession requires an internal stamina for experimentation. Susan's tenacity and commitment to excellent work resulted in a series of career tests ranging from print journalism to broadcast news.

Two Hong Kong accomplishments stand out: production of a series of live broadcasts from Seoul, South Korea, during the government slush fund scandal, and her coverage of the Hong Kong handover to Chinese rule. The undercurrent of human behavior and historical happenings fed Susan's hunger for finding stories.

Unscheduled Destination: Burnout

While in Hong Kong, Susan tipped the scales of overwork and exhaustion. To resolve questions about the future, rediscover her passion, and claim control of her life, she left her job.

With burnout as her catalyst, she shaved her head, traveled to Thailand, and set out to reimagine her life.

Burnout awareness is essential for self-correction. The wise rules of self-care and reflection make room for the zigzags required to heal and reestablish balance. Ideally this is done gradually, as there can be a dark side to following your passion with an unstoppable pace.

At the beginning of the chapter, I mentioned well-being as a key performance indicator for agile career management. As part of the happiness filter, the self-care habits of astute workers will incorporate notions of regroup, rethink, and restore as part of their daily regimens. This can be accomplished through meditation, working out, and time management.

Like athletes who train intensely to perfect their performance and increase endurance, restorative behavior improves overall results.

Susan's recovery from burnout emerged in Thailand with a deliberate mix of self-awareness, much-needed rest, and curiosity for the next stage of her creative career. With an eye toward Toronto and a worldly edge in her demeanor, she traveled west with a renewed commitment to write her way to her next endeavor.

A Through Z Testing

For Susan, story drives everything. As an instinctive storyteller, she reflected, "Follow the emotional heat and honesty. Whatever you find interesting, readers find interesting."

The versatility of Susan's mindset, along with foundational writing skills, broadened her opportunities. She mastered the boundary-blasting technique of trying new things.

After leaving Hong Kong, she worked in Toronto, Chicago, New York, and Silicon Valley. The magical thread of curiosity and growth link the roles from A to Z: on-air contributor, reporter, producer, film reviewer, copywriter, creative writer, book launch public relations, communications director, film producer, film journalist, voice-over work, social ventures consultant, and early stage urban renewal investor.

Whew! Commitment to experiences has indeed uncovered her passions. As Susan mused, "I did every job in journalism I could." Yes, I believe she has. And then some.

Susan's A/B testing chops facilitated her involvement with early stage companies, where she frequently exited the companies with a personal profit. With sage story-telling wit, she developed a voice for global companies and publications.

Susan is currently the CEO of an artificial intelligence company using blockchain technology to mine the news.

Set the Stage for the Right Moves

The advantage of A/B testing is learning from your experiences, successes, and mistakes by claiming a fresh start. With each new start, you arrive at the table with an enlightened point of view.

A New Beginning

After numerous interviews with a cast of characters, interlaced with long, silent pauses in communication, you receive the gift of a job offer from your ideal company. You've done your due diligence by researching the industry, the company, and the corporate culture. The employees and company leaders have answered your questions and appear to score high on the happiness scale.

Your first day is filled with a sense of purpose and pent-up enthusiasm. Your clean slate status is seductive. You set the tone for "all's right with the world" and plan for positive outcomes.

Now that you are in, let the games—er, work—begin.

It Starts on Day One

What happens next should resemble more of a chess game than *Game of Thrones*. Even if you have a lethal boss, abandoning impulse and intrigue to adopt clever, studied moves will serve you well.

Now is the time to set up the parameters of your test. Start on day one. With your key performance indicators of creativity, growth, and happiness established, you can steer the ship in the direction of your choosing.

The Career Hypothesis

Students and life learners seek education as a conduit for discovery of the right stuff for career callings. Talents emerge in a formal learning environment of rich research and abundant exploration. While some education tracks lead to clear-cut job descriptions, other professional routes are riddled with choice anxiety. Regardless of the training background, all individuals arrive at the starting gate of a first job, yearning for a positive experience.

In structured A/B testing throughout the course of your career, the hypothesis starts with: Job A is a good or great job. As you develop and build the role, you make adjustments to accommodate details like boredom, change, or lack of progress. You apply agile career principles to fully optimize job A's potential for creativity, growth, and happiness.

You continue to pose questions: Do I like this job? Am I attracted to a different role? What am I learning? Do I need more training? How can I make this job better? You explore your strengths and start to create preferences for certain activities. One job may be a poor fit. Another position feels like the stars are aligned with your life's work.

As you evolve, your role becomes misaligned. You may outgrow your current position. Catching the next wave of experience, Job B may be the result of a parallel pursuit or a new opportunity that catches your eye within your burgeoning network. You revise the statement to: Job B is better.

The career hypothesis is altered to accommodate the rhythm of your growth and appetite for expansion. The Agile Career Development Model illustrates the fluid figure eight pattern of career movement.

CAREER AGILITY MODEL

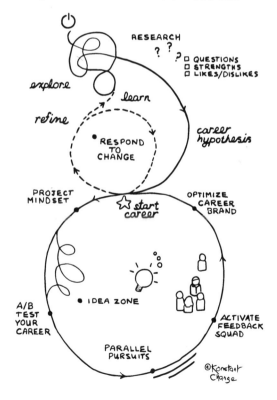

Adventures in Measurement

A/B testing and analyzing what is best for you requires measurement.

The clever attribute of measurement is the inherent ability to monitor the progress toward triumph. Using business performance measurement as an example, metrics allow enterprises to make the best use of strategy, decision making, learning, and information. Metrics such as sales, revenue, costs of goods sold, and profits are classic indicators that let businesses know they are on the right path.

When employees and entrepreneurs chart a unique course throughout their careers, personal measurement is, well, personal. Each individual possesses an inner gauge, aligning the magnetic needle of his own compass for direction.

Whether you are starting your first job or this is your tenth role, how do you determine whether this is the right job for you? Measurement!

What Should You Measure?

The Agile Career Development Model assumes the goal of our life's work is to optimize creativity, growth, and happiness. Applying these three filters in our measurement dashboard illuminates the insights to inform thoughtful decisions.

Consider the career strength trilogy as the well-being balance formula for desired performance. When negative forces weaken any of the elements, the career foundation starts to erode. Fortunately, the systematic application of agile career principles, like parallel pursuits or the Idea Zone, provides an antidote for total collapse.

How Do You Measure Creativity, Growth, and Happiness?

Unlike business metrics, such as sales, loss, and profits, the triad of well-being traits is best measured by your internal evaluation system. Of course, there are assessment tools and surveys to measure these characteristics, and you can certainly calculate your scores.

A benchmark set of results may help as a point of comparison. However, many of the tools compare populations of people and are biased by corporate definitions and regional cultures. The results will differ from criteria set by you for your career.

For example, only you can determine the state of your own happiness. Self-reporting leads to reasonable results. If given a scale of one to ten, with ten being extremely happy, most people can pick a number on the scale.

Two things define your place on the spectrum of each characteristic: your gut feeling of rank, as shown earlier in the chapter with the A/B test grid, and your responses to sample questions.

Creativity Measurement

The assumption for the Agile Careerist Development Model is creativity finds its own form of expression. Most people are creative. Yet when factors like stress and negativity permeate your existence, creative forces retreat. Your creative reservoir is dependent on an active Idea Zone, a fundamental agile careerist principle.

Consider some of the following questions and comments as you take the temperature on your creativity levels:

1. Describe what inspires you.

2. When you were eight or nine years old, what did you want to do that you have not done yet? Provide details.

3. What creative activities do you participate in? Gardening, inventive cooking, making things, tinkering with equipment, keeping a photo journal, sketching ideas in a notebook, studying architecture, writing stories, taking a dance class, woodworking, and film studies are all examples.

4. How often do you create and/or explore?

5. What are your hobbies? How do they make you feel?

6. How many responses do you generate when faced with a problem?

7. Are you willing to remove barriers and constraints from your solutions when asked to solve a problem?

8. Do you track your ideas, big or small, and revisit them regularly?

9. Are you generating new ideas on a regular basis? How often?

10. How often do you explore other disciplines like science, medicine, or mathematics to solve problems within your own discipline?

11. What do you read or what activities do you engage in to get inspired?

Growth Measurement

The Agile Careerist Development Model expects forward movement and productive work flows as functions of growth. Incremental growth achieved through deliberate and frequent steps contributes to steady career advancement.

Growth assumes a learning ethos, where expansion of skills and a sharpened mind lead to a consistent progression of responsibility and polished satisfaction. When an agile careerist notices a hint of boredom, actions are taken to evolve the role.

When Susan Oh held every observable journalism job in her purview, she peeled back the layers of the field with the dogged pursuit of a world-class gymnast. She stuck the landing and mastered her moves, taking calculated risks to uncover the truth of her work. Like the height-measurement notches of youth, where progress is marked on a visual yardstick, Susan's personal and professional growth nourished her mind and soul.

Susan also navigated the side roads of restoration to settle her fatigue. Recalibration is an important part of the story because growth is not linear. Although she made significant progress with her growth measure, she wisely assessed the decline of creativity and happiness levels. Like the triathlete who must adjust to replenish the deficits, she learned burnout will descend if proper rest and recovery are not integrated into her life.

The levels of growth are self-determined according to your goals and personality. Like your unique definition of success, you define your particular definition of growth markers.

Following are some questions and comments to ponder as you quantify and track your growth progress:

1. Describe the roles you have held in your current line of work.

2. Define the times you saw a need in the company and filled the gap with your talents.

3. How many times did you take on a less-than-desirable role to support company goals?

3. What types of training have you participated in to further your skills?

4. Have your added any skills to your portfolio?

5. Is the study of leadership integrated into your workplan?

6. Have you engaged in any parallel pursuits to further your knowledge and/or satisfy your curiosity?

7. Are you being rewarded financially for your progress?

8. Does your growth strategy consider the balance of life and work?

9. Do you take responsibility for your own growth by actively pursuing work and projects that interest you?

10. Are you self-directed when it comes to your workday and job responsibilities?

11. Looking back, how have you improved?

12. What procedures did you use to address setbacks and challenges?

13. Is integrity a part of your work demeanor? With yourself and with others?

14. Do you give of yourself in the workplace for others to benefit? Provide examples.

Happiness Measurement
Scores of authors and neuroscience advocates have studied happiness because of its integral role in personal health

and the well-being of our planet. A TED Talk elaborated on the happiest places on earth as measured by Happy Planet Index (HPI). The country of Bhutan measures Gross National Happiness. As a reader of happiness books, this makes me smile, and I am grateful the topic of happiness is trending.

While not an expert on the many studies of happiness, the stark difference between my own dark sadness and luxurious happiness is evident. When a deep funk rolls in like a spring thunderstorm, happiness is hidden. In contrast to the frustration of work's dark times, joyful work possesses the exalted status of contentment and renewed energy.

The happiness zone within our life's work provisions the pipeline for creativity and growth, reinforcing the interdependent triumvirate of the Agile Career Development Model. The model includes happiness because it is the backbone of our dreams.

Feeling compelled to share a happiness tale, I offer you an Irish gem about a storyteller in action.

The Happiness Whisperer

The story starts in a family Irish import store on the Northwest side of Chicago when Noeleen McGrath was in fifth grade. Her siblings commanded attention with their visible personalities. Her brother was the life of the party, while her extroverted sister's persuasive ability to sell anything to anyone often took center stage. As the quiet one, Noeleen earned the reputation of listener at the checkout counter of the store.

As she said, "There was something about the stories. Sometimes people came to the store just to talk." She learned to read people quickly and encouraged them to confide in her with their stories. Her forte for eliciting trust and delightful stories was her genuine interest.

Noeleen excelled in the happiness response intertwined with fierce grit when she started in on-air TV news while in college. She worked in the Chicago bureau for CNN as a producer, achieving the status of local news anchor reporter. Painfully shy as a child, she conquered her fear when she mastered public speaking and was noticed by one of her professors.

With her vivid blue eyes and dazzling smile, Noeleen commanded attention with her confidence and honest presence. By the time Noeleen was twenty-one, she had amassed a significant amount of exposure in the business.

The business of broadcast news is hyper-competitive. When all the internships were assigned at CNN, she participated in a "no chance" interview. Her interviewer chatted with her because he was polite, even though there were no more openings. She hung in there with all the attitude and chutzpah of a positive mental attitude devotee. Later in the day, the manager called to tell her he reorganized the lineup to recruit her for his team.

Her ready-for-anything attitude served her well as she navigated her intern responsibilities. Noeleen was producing stories as a freelancer within one month of her internship, while still a junior in college.

She approaches her happiness from the inside out as she celebrates the success of others. In her words, "I cheer for the people who win on game shows. I celebrate the success of my clients. I cheer for the people who win!"

As a producer, Noeleen prepared the mountains of work and fact-gathering backstories. With limited on-air experience, the desire to tell her stories derived from countless interviews while working as a producer.

She once endured sabotage from a fellow worker and a broken monitor during a live broadcast in front of the camera as a local news reporter anchor. In spite of the absent teleprompter content, she put her stunning memory skills to the test. Noeleen conducted a flawless broadcast with a smile.

She steered clear of calling out the undermining activity of her coworker. In an imperfect world, her persevering nature and happy demeanor win the awards. She earned a Murrow Award, the outstanding achievement for electronic journalism, a reflection of her hard work. The biggest accomplishment for Noeleen, however, was her steadfast focus in the face of formidable pressure. Makes me want to grab a bit of happiness and cheer for people who win!

After twelve years in TV news, she felt she was being dragged down by negativity in the industry and instead chose a career path with happiness potential. She now works as an independent media trainer for corporations, executives, and legal teams, coaching others how to handle the pressure of on-air filming, especially in times of crisis.

Explore Your Happiness Meter

During the Agile Careerist Project, I observed some people are wired for happiness and others put more effort into achieving happiness. The common truth is no one is capable of sustaining this pleasant state of mind indefinitely.

A common technique among happiness seekers is the gratitude journal habit. This was a project made popular by Oprah Winfrey and Sarah Ban Breathnach, the author of *The Simple Abundance Journal of Gratitude*. In the workbook, readers wrote three things they were grateful for each day, ending the day with a grateful heart.

Among the three agile careerist attitudes, happiness is perhaps the easiest to measure, by simply answering the question, "Am I happy?" The key, however, is in the habits included in the following questions:

1. Are you happy with your current work situation?
2. Have you considered keeping a gratitude journal?
3. Do you look forward to going to work?
4. Are you working on any projects that hold your attention and interest?
5. What is your experience when you collaborate with others for the purpose of working toward a shared goal?
6. Is helping others at work part of your daily habits?
7. Do you share credit for accomplishments?
8. Are there other attractive roles in your present company?
9. What are your accomplishments?
10. Name your proudest work accomplishment. Are you working on projects similar to that now or in the near future?
11. Could you be happier somewhere else?
12. Is your current role a bad fit?

Next Steps

A/B testing starts with a career hypothesis. Using this method for measuring your satisfaction leads to the systematic evolution of pursuing work you want to do vs. what you are doing now. Have you thought about setting up a testing environment, inviting change and the possibility of more fulfilling work?

Pick one tactic from the current list to use as a barometer for liking your current job role:

1. Conduct an audit of the trio of career attributes mentioned earlier in the chapter: creativity, growth, and happiness. Are you in balance? You can use the list of questions within each section of this chapter.

2. Make a list of accessible job opportunities aligned with your current work that fit growth parameters. Refine the list by asking whether you might prefer one of these opportunities to your current role.

3. If you are engaged in a side gig or side hustle, apply the filters of creativity, growth, and happiness potential to determine whether or how you could move forward.

4. If there were no barriers, what job would you consider instead of your current role? Research whether there is a viable version of this scenario.

CHAPTER 5

Principle Four:
Respond to Change

Change is inevitable. Progress is optional.
—TONY ROBBINS, ENTREPRENEUR,
AUTHOR, PHILANTHROPIST,
LIFE/BUSINESS STRATEGIST

In Sync With Change

As a cornerstone of the Agile Career Development Model, the Respond to Change Principle advances the agility meter with full throttle motion. The drum roll and happy dance combine when the cool, calm, collected agile worker maneuvers through and around the obstacle course called employment. The take charge fundamental is embedded within all other agile career principles, making it possible to thrive in the workplace.

Respond to Change Principle

Acceleration of technology and continuous state of change calls for flexibility and willingness to adapt. Lean into change and make adjustments to your career status, rather than sticking to a rigid plan. Acclimate to economic developments and corporate adjustments by uncovering engaging projects. Discover market and employment gaps you can fulfill in a unique manner.

When change is circulating around you, this is your go-to principle, showing others you are in control when the world gets dicey and unpredictable. If you had to adopt just one facet from the model, invite the superfood of principles into your survival kit. Take it one step further by turning it into your "thrival" playbook. Keep it at the ready for easy access.

Acceleration of technology and a continuous state of change signal the urgent need for employee flexibility and the workforce's willingness to adapt. Professional plans are subject to change due to uncertain circumstances. Fluid career systems responding to change, not rigid plans, align with personal and corporate goals.

This chapter will help you integrate a Respond to Change mindset into your personal career navigation algorithm. Because change is a recurring element in the work environment, it is advantageous to anticipate, rather than avoid, the inevitable disturbances to the status quo.

Through sharing compelling stories and workplace observations, we will examine various types of change, paired with ideas for decisive action. The goal of this chapter is to establish a productive awareness of inflection points throughout your career. The insights offered will help you manage the dynamic developments of your life's work.

We will also study change's trusty sidekick, uncertainty, and its influence in updating or revising job roles. Let's also remember fear, an unrelenting companion of change and uncertainty.

Change, Uncertainty, and Fear walked into a bar . . .
Let's get started with change.

Sense and Respond

When I was in business school, a perceptive coach advisor offered powerful advice to our product development lab students. We were an unruly seven-person team, attempting to gel as a global cohort of business students. The project was requested by a Fortune 500 client and included market analysis, product development, and marketing strategy. We struggled mightily with meeting client needs at pivotal presentation points during the six-month project.

Our coach counseled—or rather, admonished—us to keep our eyes and ears on the client members while delivering a report, adopting a "sense and respond" strategy. He suggested connecting with the corporate managers during the presentation, while concurrently monitoring their reactions. He recommended consistent eye contact, observation of body language, and paying close attention to client questions.

This approach enabled dynamic, nuanced adjustments, better serving and relating to the business group who invested in our group's research and recommendations.

Our student team recovered under the coach's guidance as we assumed control of the dashboard levers. The sense and respond directive created an observant vision of change that included market forces, competitor actions, and customer needs.

While long-term career management is more complex than presenting a customer solution, awareness of changes in the environment uncovers crucial issues. Awareness leads to thoughtful analysis, conscious decisions, and rewarding outcomes.

Futurist, Starter, Builder, and Fixer

During the summer of 2010, I set out to uncover human pockets of technology development and creativity to define Chicago's tech ecosystem. While working as a chief marketing officer at a mobile security company, I wanted to invigorate my predictable problem-solving patterns with a technology trends refresh.

When I posed the question, "Who could best define the tech ecosystem in Chicago?" a friend of mine quickly suggested the name Howard Tullman, offering an introduction. Howard is a charismatic leader and wildly successful entrepreneur who launched and nurtured over a dozen businesses in Chicago. He sold a few of them for hundreds of millions of dollars.

Howard was then CEO and cofounder of Tribeca Flashpoint Media Arts Academy, a skills-based digital college preparing students for jobs in the multimedia world.

If the Midwest work ethic were paired with a symbolic icon, Howard Tullman, with his signature wavy, gray ponytail, engaging smile, and no-nonsense piercing gaze, would be a top candidate for the spot.

While in Howard's office for my first meeting, the sensory explosion of past projects and a Rolling Stones iconic tongue logo poster flickered before me. His walls and desk were packed with artifacts of whimsy, classic success stories, and digital prototype concepts. The concert and movie prints in the corridors beckoned a hallway explorer into a vortex of time travel from the 1970s music history through current-day Hollywood. Howard's forte for popular culture and the creative arts was my first clue regarding his innate talent for trend detection.

Cultivating Change at the Edge of Innovation

Howard's Respond to Change reflex serves as a market opportunity amplifier. He invites change into his fearless, business-blending brain. He synthesizes it to create something new, fix something broken, or build something bigger.

Innovation and change created an elixir to be consumed while conversing with Howard Tullman. I witnessed his fiery curiosity and commitment to the edge of innovation, guided by pragmatic project management and real-world business skills. He brought up two topics that are ubiquitous now, but not so much in 2010:

- Internet of Things (IoT). Howard surmised technology devices and clothing would play a role in digital interaction with our environment.

- Augmented Reality (AR). He suggested advertisers would make use of this technology by greeting people at the screen of their choice. This was six years prior to the Pokemon GO augmented reality gaming sensation.

Glimpsing a Respond to Change aptitude as agile as Howard Tullman's visionary mentality provoked me to sharpen my vision of trends and boundless possibilities. Detecting what's possible, and combining it with trends, surely includes membership in the plugged-in club of progressive business thinkers. Howard would be awarded a lifetime membership in this club.

Change Agent to Change Synthesizer

Six years later, in 2016, when I interviewed Howard Tullman in a modern glass-walled conference room, he was CEO of

1871, Chicago's entrepreneurial hub for digital startups. His relationship with change and disruptive innovation shapes the elements of his "builder" philosophy.

Howard's razor-sharp interaction with change enables him to gain advantage, especially when a business is in trouble or a new technology emerges. He works as a change agent *and* a change responder.

The Respond to Change Principle encourages people to do two things:

1. Notice the change

2. Take action

These two instructions are required, in spite of fear or uncertainty. Ah yes, the trusty sidekick of change will happily drink anyone under the table to occasionally derail necessary actions. Similar to the sense and respond advice from my business school advisor, the applied principle allows you to take control, rather than be a passive bystander.

You can respond as a business leader, as in steering the ship of a business venture as Howard does, or as an individual directing his career story. Here are four examples of how Howard Tullman observed trends and responded to change at a macro level in his business leader role. In all of them, Howard's unstoppable nature outmaneuvers predictable fear, leaving it in the dust while he reconciles uncertainty and leverages change.

Disruptive Innovation and CCC Information Services
In 1980, after working ten years as a trial lawyer, Howard started his first company, CCC Information Services. Howard noticed the technology developments and power of business computing at a time when managing data equated to

organizing Excel spreadsheet data. He saw lots of information ready to be accessed and systematized like never before. Regardless of the uncertain nature of doing something never before accomplished, he developed the first database to be used in class action lawsuits.

The company migrated its competency in legal databases to the automotive and insurance businesses, two industries aching for better-organized data. CCC revolutionized these industries to consider customer satisfaction and lifetime value of a customer. The company went public in 1983 and was sold for over $100 million in 1987, a significant deal at the time. In 2017, CCC, reportedly valued at $3 billion by Bloomberg, was acquired by Advent International. Database management aggressively transformed these two sluggish industries. Howard saw the influence of big data before systems were designed to manage facts and figures.

Turnaround of Kendall College

Two seemingly unrelated facts, reflecting the winds of change in 2003, were apparent when Howard took over as CEO of Kendall College. The school, a nonprofit institution, was failing, and the restaurant industry was in growth mode. Howard responded to these trends by turning Kendall into a for-profit school focused on culinary arts and business education. He cut slower-growth curriculum and eliminated athletics. He moved the campus from suburban Evanston to a contemporary facility in a hip neighborhood in the city. A turnaround success story, the school was sold in 2008 for over $300 million.

The Age of Mastery at Tribeca Flashpoint

Three trends were evident when Howard decided to launch a new type of school:

- Mastery of skills was a way to claim relevance in the work world, thanks in part to the influential writings of Malcolm Gladwell.

- There was a gap between job demand and availability of digitally skilled practitioners in the media arts, a growth business.

- Many college students were bored with their studies in conventional universities and did not like their area of study.

In 2007, Howard responded by founding Tribeca Flashpoint College, a digital media school, where he changed the high-end vocational education model. The school's graduates are fully capable of doing the work of filmmakers, animators, and recording artists. Howard believes in the 100 percent rule. Many students today graduate with less than 80 percent of what is needed to do the work. According to Howard, "If we built a house that is 80 percent right, it would fall down."

Resetting the Course of 1871, Technology Incubator

1871 represents the year of the Great Fire and the Chicago response when the city made bold plans, rebuilding itself into an architectural mecca and business center. The naming of the nonprofit tech hub 1871 epitomizes the grit and perseverance of a ravaged community, a city that emerged from the devastating fire and ashes. And the belief technology will drive a new renaissance for Chicago.

When Howard took over leadership at 1871, there were two issues: it was not profitable, and business leaders were drawn to the cultivation of promising startups. He responded by:

- Creating an "up or out" mandate for the resident startups, with a goal of nurturing businesses with sustainable business models

- Adding multiple lines of revenue: events, education, rent, sponsorship, programs, consulting, and donations. He made it clear 1871's business model could not be dependent on any one thing.

- Focusing on business-to-business, a core competency of the region

The organization is profitable and is 300 to 400 percent larger than when he started. Over 250 companies have graduated; other companies were moved up or out. 1871 created over 7,000 jobs and raised $200–$225 million for its companies.

Howard will stay at 1871 as long as progressive change and substantive growth are present. He makes the distinction "not pure growth" but rather an environment where new thinking, systems, and processes drive change. He moves on when "building" is complete, the operation is steady, and the organization is in need of the next phase of management.

If the Times Are a-Changing, So Should You

With over forty-five years of business experience, Howard Tullman's roles as serial entrepreneur and agile business leader demonstrate his voluntary alliance with change. Viewing change as an opportunity, he attacks uncertain circumstances with the dexterity of a nimble hockey player.

Whether you are an entrepreneur, employee, executive, or front line worker, it's your turn to place the welcome mat in full view of change. Consider inviting change into your career compass calculations for your own advantage. Let's outline the various dimensions of change, and then we will greet the vexing characters of fear and uncertainty. I know some of you might be thinking:

- I want something better, but I don't want to upset my life or my family.

- Every time I get ready to make a powerful decision, fear gets in the way.

- My industry is collapsing, and I wonder whether it's possible to move to another industry or another role.

- There are so many new developments and uncertainty in the business environment, I don't know where to focus.

- The business models in my industry have changed, and my role will become obsolete; it's not a matter of if, but when.

- My boss is impossible, but maybe he will leave and I can stay at my current job; my job isn't that bad. It's the job I know.

- I've been passed over for a promotion, and new management is moving in.

- There is so much change going on out there, I don't know how to respond.

- Quitting right now is the best thing. I will figure out next steps later.

- Maybe I should start a business, since working for corporations does not agree with me.

Dimensions of Change

Fear of descending down Alice's infamous rabbit hole keeps some of us in place, until something happens to us. Sound familiar? Sneaky change happens and we react, rather than take strategic action. Now it is an urgent crisis demanding attention instead of a deliberate choice.

Let's review change from macro and micro perspectives. Macro developments affect everyone, whereas micro change is specific to you, the individual. This list is an example of the types of influences that impact business professionals today.

Macro Influence

Macro changes, like the 2008 Global Financial Crisis or the technology trend keeping us tethered to our "always on" devices, affect us all. The same is true for advancements in science or the globalization of our economy. Each of these elements is part of a complex interdependent system, in a constant state of evolution.

Discerning observers of patterns and trends, like Howard Tullman, develop novel ideas inspired by industry shifts or gaping voids. He assimilated change, noticed what was missing, and actively planned to engage with technology advancements.

Howard Tullman's Response to Change Principle in Action

Macro change:

Computing technology advancements and data were in disarray, growing every day with only spreadsheets as a method of organization

Response:

Organize data by creating computer-based solutions to sort and analyze important business assets and information

With every change, negative or positive, there is an opportunity to respond by taking command of the driver's seat, rather than as a passive rider. Disciplined career management enables you to create the rules, rather than be pulled in the direction of a reckless storm.

Like the agile crew steering a sailboat on a gusty day, the macro changes of the unpredictable wind and moody water highlight macro changes affecting the sport. These changes must be reconciled to cross the water or win the race. In response, the team moves forward with the wind at their backs or zigzags against it, using the headwind to propel in the opposite direction of the breeze.

You might be thinking, "What are some practical examples of macro change and how do people respond? And how do individuals wrestle the three-headed monster of change, fear, and uncertainty?"

Macro Change: The Mobile Workplace

Looking through the list of trends, let's contemplate the ascent of the mobile workforce empowered by portable devices and online tools. The macro change includes mobility and cloud-based business services. The responses to this trend have exploded into abundant work options for corporations and individuals.

Employee mobility represented a substantial change in the workplace and was often looked upon with suspicion. The downside translated to the on-call expectation between employer and employee. Fears regarding work-life balance burst onto the employee list of concerns. Senior leaders eyed the prize of deploying a mobility strategy to their best advantage, facilitating the delicate balance between productivity and privacy.

The promise of flexible work arrangements, however, loomed as the largest benefit for professionals. It wasn't long before we reflected, "Where have all the desktop computers gone?" The following example provides a glimpse.

Whose Virtual Reality is This?

Macro Change:

Mobile Device Availability and Online Collaboration Tools
Response:

The Birth of the Virtual Team and Rise of Virtual Companies
In 1999, Jason Fried launched 37signals, a web design

company that evolved into a productivity tools company, Basecamp. The company's web-based collaboration tools are used by millions across the globe and enable interaction among teams, regardless of their location.

Because Jason's company espouses the value of productivity, he feels managers should have access to the best available team members. As many consulting firms and corporations have demonstrated, the best available players are not always at the same office. Location independence is an essential requirement for certain projects.

Jason created Basecamp, a virtual company, where employees live in different regions yet are able to collaborate as an integrated team. The local Chicago people have access to an office, yet are not required to work in the office. Remote workers include local residents and those scattered across the world. The company exemplifies the exact benefits of their product through their daily interaction with each other.

Basecamp extends the virtual collaborative workspace to individuals and businesses worldwide. Distributed teams and virtual companies are outcomes of the mobility trend, made possible by two things: mobile devices and pioneering project collaboration tools.

The Untethered Pro

Let's look at an additional response to the macro change surrounding mobility and online tools.

Macro Change:

Mobile Device Availability and Online Collaboration Tools
Response:

Digital Nomads, Solopreneurs, Freelance Gigs, and Corporate Remote Offices

The chain reaction accompanying the mobility trend has intensified the solopreneur and freelance movements.

The phrase "digital nomad" materialized in recent years, referring to an individual who travels to assorted domestic or foreign locations while accomplishing their projects. This group likes to travel, collaborate with people from different cultures, and ensure their global relevance for future employment. Their work product is created via a computer, wireless services, and web-based tools. They work out of coworking spaces, coffee shops, and places with Wi-Fi hotspot connections.

Do you know someone who works this way? You might subscribe to their intriguing blog. Surprisingly, millennials, news correspondents, and National Geographic photographers are not the only participants in this nomadic work culture. For example, various third-stage professionals like boomers who desire international experiences, structure their businesses in a similar fashion.

This new professional breed of workers did not wait for the future to happen in their current jobs. They invited macro change through the front door and hatched an original work mode. Companies and employees who viewed mobility as an opportunity leveraged the change through progressive discovery of new ways to work and live in the global frontier.

When a Fortune 100 company acquired the mobile security startup where I was an executive, we were not required to move across the country to corporate headquarters. Our eight-person staff worked remotely, even after the local office closed. All made possible by technology systems and networks.

Many corporations welcome the mobile devices but struggle to sanction the release of the global employee from the fixed environment. Like people, businesses are also victim to fear and uncertainty. They value a more conservative onsite requirement to workplace productivity than Jason Fried's remote worker flexibility.

Individuals have figured out the dividing line separating work and home and are more thoroughly optimizing the flexibility of their mobile environments, especially when they are on the road. And no matter how large the organization, there will always be a need for effective distributed teams.

Macro Change: Technology Innovation

Now that we have reviewed the impact of mobility on our work habits, let's examine another macro change from our earlier list. The acceleration of technology, like the steady flow of river rapids, fluctuates between fluid movement and a turbulent current. Perpetual movement. We can scarcely remember when computers, online interaction, and the incessant progression of apps were not part of our daily ritual.

Admit it, when you leave the house without your mobile phone, do you feel unprepared for your day? Do you worry important events are happening without your knowledge? Mobile devices have become an extension of our exclusive memory banks and play the role of a reliable personal assistant.

While we have electronically incorporated technology resources into our lives, the majority of people in the workforce today are not considered digital natives. Born between 1995 and 2015, Generation Z is the first population of truly digital beings, interacting with computers since birth. Their collective response to technology has not yet been felt in the work landscape.

When Gen Z came of age to tote their first mobile device, it was a smartphone, the world's tiniest computer, rather than a cellphone designed to talk voice-to-voice. Neuroscientists have suggested the human brain is being rewired to conform to the deluge of information fluttering across our field of vision. For example, short bursts of visual content are more valued by this generation than text-based messages. Attention spans for the written word are short.

The three generations presently in the workplace have experienced astonishing technology shifts throughout their careers. Various boomers and Gen Xers interviewed in the Agile Careerist Project expressed concerns regarding keeping up with the technology side of their job.

While older employees possess a great amount of industry knowledge necessary for corporations to function, organizations demand technical fluency. Older workers fear the permanent beat of new learning systems and processes snapping at their heels.

Disruptive technologies like driverless cars and artificial intelligence will continue to transform how we think and live. The changes driven by these developments compel workers to adapt or get left behind, regardless of fear or uncertainty. As Gen Z advances into the workplace, the acceleration of change will, indeed, be a wild ride.

Resilience of The Adaptable Educator

Macro Change:

Technology Acceleration Across Industries

Response:

Reinvent Roles Based on Technology

In 1995, Colleen Cannon-Ruffo, a high school Spanish teacher with a quick smile and hearty laugh, made a decision. She decided to get a master's degree in instructional technology. When the world's first internet boom shattered the conventional workplace, Colleen assessed technology was about to transform the education profession.

With limited resources, Colleen created learning modules for her Spanish students, including web-based activities and software-based projects. Her unvarnished enthusiasm for the creative realm behind the computer screen was contagious.

Her attitude, accompanied by animated, curly brown hair, was infused with energy. As one of the youngest teachers in her school, unconstrained by historical habits, she initiated a maker mentality for students throughout her course design. To strengthen learning potential, students created digital artifacts, reflecting their retained knowledge of required subject matter. She encouraged class participants to share stories combining language and technology. The students flourished in the new world of computer projects as an expression of artistry and digital proficiency.

A big problem emerged—the unintended consequences of innovative thinking. The other teachers were not as adept as Colleen and were resistant to following her lead in their own classrooms. She desired to help solve the problem by extending computer acumen to other faculty. Colleen was convinced students would thrive in a technology-enhanced instruction setting, using software tools disguised as enjoyable games.

She qualified as one of the first instructors in a train the trainers program for instructors at Argonne National Laboratory. She coached educators, the very same teachers intimidated by technology integration in their classrooms. Her vision of the future classroom instilled the promise of immense growth for young minds.

By 2005, Colleen reconstructed her newly formed position from classroom teacher to technology integration within the teaching curriculum. For several years, she juggled classroom responsibilities with after-hours educator tech training. Her patience paid off when her district invited her to apply for a newly created role in instructional technology.

The new role enabled her to help teachers mitigate their fears and apply technology in the classroom. The job activities included curriculum design, computer and software evaluation, and technology implementation. Her most pressing work, however, was to evolve her pioneering role while selling new ideas to administrators and teachers. As she said, "I was learning and delivering the program at the same time." Colleen's curious relationship with uncertainty fosters a mindset of "test and explore ideas" while solving pop-up problems as they arise.

Colleen's favorite professional obligation is functioning as an idea architect for classroom projects. Working as a coach in the computer labs, she facilitates fearless students who bring robots to life with their coding skills. As she mused, "With the youngest kids, I just watch. They start right away, minimizing the need for lengthy instructional time." Digital natives, capable of intuitive self-direction, will indeed change the learning landscape.

As she completes her PhD in Instructional Technology, Colleen's next career chapter will include abundant imaginative responses to technology advancement.

Micro Influence and Response to Change

Now that we've explored a few examples of how individuals respond to macro change, let's reflect on how people respond to micro influences. Macro developments affect everyone, whereas micro change is specific to you.

CAREER MICRO INFLUENCES

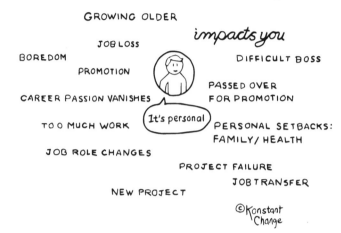

Micro change feels personal. You may be in a difficult place where your boss is increasingly unreasonable or crazy. Maybe you were passed over for a promotion. Or your job function was eliminated and you are scrambling to find a new position, rather than moving forward in a deliberate career management mode.

There are other developments close to you that are less personal, yet no less disruptive. A change in corporate structure or a new department project can have ripple effects from the highest levels in the organization all the way to you.

Direct-impact change can feel like an earthquake, affecting the stability of your life and the ground where you plant your feet. Dreams dashed in an instant. It can also feel like a dream-stealing headache, where a steady drip of negative influences erodes at the core. You may become witness to a slow-motion movie flop in an infinite loop, playing over and over and over again.

The three guys at the bar—Change, Uncertainty, and Fear—can become dangerously close to dominating the reel in your head.

But wait—responding with arms akimbo in a power stance accompanied by an "I mean business" look, will enact the Respond to Change Principle. With a take-control attitude, this principle becomes the advocate for your life's work as you calculate what's next.

Following are a couple examples of how some professionals responded to change.

The Roving Podcaster Tells a Viral Story

Micro Change:

Passed Over For a Promotion in the TV News Business

Response:

Become an Entrepreneur; Create a Self-Produced Podcast Series

In the summer of 2016, an article caught my eye regarding one of my favorite local TV news reporters at NBC, Anthony Ponce. In a viral Facebook post viewed over one million times, Anthony announced his decision to leave his post as a general assignment reporter to create a podcast series called *Backseat Rider*.

After being passed over twice for a promotion, he decided to leave his TV reporter role. He had been driving a Lyft car as a research experiment, in parallel with his reporter role, when he made his final decision to focus on this creative idea.

The podcast series features Anthony in the driver's seat of a Lyft vehicle recording conversations with backseat riders about current events, life's anecdotes, and personal stories. He embraces the "driver as storyteller" concept as an entrepreneurial experiment, and intends to figure out the business side of podcasting. Within six months of launch, *Backseat Rider* was picked up and distributed via PodCastOne, a leading on-demand digital audio network.

The practical side of making money is never far from the reality check of making a living. From ride sharing to story sharing, Anthony intends to explore conversations beyond the traditional ten-second sound bites of TV news.

Yes She Can

Micro Change:

Dismissive Executive Discourages New College Recruit

Response:

Rise to the Top

First in her family to go to college, Janet Viane, a baby boomer, grew up in a blue-collar environment. Hard work and resilience were incorporated into the survival kit for ambitious neighborhood kids.

Her father died when she was four years old. Her mother lacked a formal education. A mother's sage wisdom, however, offered Janet valuable advice: be inclusive and embrace people with differences. Her mother nurtured mentally ill children in a state-funded private home, treating each of these children as part of her family. As a child, Janet learned about compassion and volunteerism as she helped her mother care for the kids who were different.

Scoring grades at the top of the scales eluded Janet. What she lacked in academic test-taking abilities was compensated for with savvy leadership, team building skills, and innate people-development talents.

One of the vice presidents at her first job at a Fortune 500 printing and publishing company told Janet she would never amount to much. He reasoned she did not attend the right school or have the best grades, and her Chicago Southside accent would be a hindrance. The hateful comments stoked the furnace in her belly. She remembers thinking, "Stay out of the way, when someone tells me I cannot do something."

Within twelve years, her stubborn denial of the executive's negative predictions resulted in six promotions within nine years, ranging from technical recruiter to vice president of human resources. Since that time, Janet has worked as a business owner, chief marketing and sales officer, chief operating officer, and CEO of a corporate division of a Fortune 100 company.

Wrestle the Dragon of Fear, Uncertainty, and Change

Responding to change is a bold move. It can be scary, yet it can also be an exhilarating experience. While all responses to change do not have to be grand gestures, as in looking the dragon in the eyes, you can start with deliberate, thoughtful observations.

A clever observer in the workforce can compel counterattacks when opposing forces make a move or when failure is imminent. The active onlooker owns the edge of awareness and can take actions to ensure a good outcome, rather than wait for the wave of inevitable doom.

Disruption can be slow and incremental or it can sweep in with a torturous roar. Regarding my own career path, there were times when I was totally blindsided by events. Like the time I walked into the office at Twenty South Riverside Plaza, ready to start my workday. After ten months on the job for a digital spinoff business, all thirty employees were rounded up into a conference room to be let go in unison by a parent company executive.

In spite of the instant unemployment status, I first responded to change with a sigh of relief. It had been a tough year working for a company plagued by helicopter parent behavior, not quite ready to let the "child" company prosper on its own terms.

My response to change resulted in obtaining a senior leadership role at a branding agency.

The theater of our life's work is flush with opportunities to respond. There is power in taking control when our firm footing is interrupted by unwelcome change. And there is satisfaction when trends are identified in preparation for making a positive career move.

Next Steps

Self-reflection, analyzing your historical career path, and reviewing your approach to change will help you explore effective ways to respond to change. Now that you have seen the Respond to Change stories of entrepreneurs and work navigators in this chapter, let's examine your potential responses to change.

Cultivating or optimizing your responses to change is not an impulsive exercise. You first need to understand your patterns and then imagine responses to change that put you in the driver's seat.

In an effort to exert conscious control of how you respond to change, complete one or two exercises from the following:

1. List the macro trends affecting your current role. Define some ideas for dealing with or optimizing this type of change. Refer to the agile career principles listed in question three.

2. List the micro trends affecting you in your workplace. Define steps for responding to these circumstances with the intention of taking charge, rather than letting the corporation make decisions. Apply the filters of creativity, growth, and

happiness as you consider your responses. Refer to the agile career principles listed in question three.

3. Review your work history. Write down a few instances of macro or micro change and your responses to the circumstances. Pick one or two of the principles that may have been used to more intentionally manage your career path. Write these ideas down. The following agile career principles featured in the previous chapters are listed for your reference:

- Create an Idea Zone
- Pursue It in Parallel
- A/B Test Your Career
- Respond to Change

CHAPTER 6

Principle Five: Optimize Your Personal Brand

Be so good they can't ignore you.
—STEVE MARTIN

Whose Life Is It, Anyway?

The lines between our work lives and personal domains have evaporated. In a flash, smartphones broke down the barriers between worlds, merging work and life into an integrated realm.

It started long before that, when pagers were clipped to our belts or stashed in our handbags. When the beeping sound crept into a family picnic or a dinner engagement, we quickly slipped into the mythical Superman phone booth, and changed into our work persona, ready for business.

Our lives alternate between pockets of work, play, and home-work, effortlessly erasing our past split personalities, forming one undeniable authentic person.

This progressive scenario, like a primer coat of paint preparing for a burst of color, opened the gates of personal definition in the workplace. We are no longer defined primarily by our job function. Our professional biographies weave together personal sparks of interest, rather than blah, blah, blah . . . yawn, the boring third-person recital of our credentials.

Which brings me to the topic of this chapter, personal branding, also known as career branding.

Principle Five: Optimize Your Personal Brand

Steve Martin's pithy quote offers significant meaning to brand creation and brand development. "Be so good they can't ignore you." The wisdom of his direct phrase illuminates a "stand out" command. In branding terms, if you are different from the rest, and visible, you are memorable. When the time comes for employers, partners, and clients to choose someone with your unique and notable qualities, you will rise to the top. You will be chosen above all others.

The optimization of your personal brand requires consistent reflection and vigilant attention. Let's revisit the principle listed in the first chapter.

Personal Brand Principle

Uncover your distinguishing characteristics or brand values. Package your portfolio of skills and be consistent in how you communicate and present yourself to the human workplace. When making a decision, pose the question: Is this in alignment with my brand values? Spread the story-driven message in real life and across your digital networks. Be bold and dare to be different.

The call of personal branding, like the call of the wild, invades the center and corners of the business universe, chiding each of us to develop a personal brand. But, what does your brand look like? How do you create one in the jungle of popular culture, where branding involves the booming presence of mega-talented Beyoncé, high-profile actors, and the crew of Kardashians?

Lucky for you, the business of career branding steers clear of the obsession with selfie-laden entertainment brands. There will be no pressure to conform to the celebrity of personalities like the *Shark Tank* retail business savant, Daymond John, or the music industry's wunderkind Taylor Swift, with eighty million Twitter followers. Career branding is much easier than the universe of superstar personalities. You can be you—the main idea, after all—rather than customizing yourself for legions of fans.

The purpose of this chapter is to:

- Provide a branding overview
- Guide you through the personal brand development process
- Help you define your personal brand
- Share stories of people who have successfully optimized their brand
- Suggest tactics for launching and optimizing your brand
- Challenge you to take control by defining and managing your value in the workplace

Employer reviews depict one facet of your value. The rest is up to you. The best place to start is to understand who you are, what you have accomplished, and what you want in the future. Maybe you are seeking a change. Or, you want to gain access to the next layer of opportunity in your current organization.

For now, let's rewind the reel to illuminate the discipline and practice of professional branding, where it all started.

The Dawning of The Corporate Brand Age

By paging through the history books of corporate evolution and their relationships with consumers, we can review some brand basics. Brands and consumer products were first made popular by the "Mad Men" of the early 1960s, a term used to describe successful advertising people who worked on Madison Avenue.

Consumer brands and the people who promote them have grown beyond those days, evolving from know-it-all personalities to listening agents. People inside companies ask the customer what she needs, rather than shout through a megaphone with their singular assumptions about what people desire.

Large consumer brands like Coca-Cola and Starbucks enable business valuation experts to price the value of a brand as a corporate asset. Organizations invest in corporate brands to increase company value, differentiate from competitors, and instill loyalty among customers. Investments occur in the form of advertising, public relations, marketing, product development, customer experience, and a montage of awareness efforts.

Companies continue to rebrand in response to business issues, like a change in strategy, declining sales, or a new product launch.

Some quotes and definitions of organizational branding include:

Brand Definition

- A brand is a promise. —*Unknown author, yet this quote has been used as the lead-in for many other quotes about brand and is an accepted universal truth by marketers*

- A brand is simply trust. —*Steve Jobs*
- A brand is a person's gut feeling about a product, service, or company. —*Marty Neumeier, author, speaker on topics of brand, design, innovation, and creativity*
- A brand is a singular idea or concept that you own inside the mind of a prospect. —*Al Reis, marketing professional, pioneer of positioning, and author*
- We use brands to project who we want to be in the world, how we want people to perceive us, and how we want to feel about ourselves. — *Debbie Millman, writer, educator, artist, design observer, and host of podcast* Design Matters
- A brand is a voice and a product is a souvenir. —*Lisa Gansky, venture investor, entrepreneur, and author of* The Mesh: Why The Future of Business is Sharing

Brand Strategy Elements

- Success doesn't come from what you do occasionally; it comes from what you do consistently. —*Marie Forleo, life/business coach, motivational speaker, author, and founder of online B-School and* MarieTV
- Whatever you do, be different. If you're different, you will stand out. —*Anita Roddick, British businesswoman, human rights activist, and founder of The Body Shop*

- Knowing where you're going is irresistibly
  attractive. —*Liz Strauss, entrepreneur, author,
  speaker, marketer, social media influencer,
  and event producer*

The most visible and attractive brands in the world, like Nike, Apple, Disney, and Google, create a human connection with their customers. As consumers, we feel better about ourselves by affiliating with these brands.

Now, what about you? How does the shaping of a business or its products relate to your career quest? Personal brand development heeds the instruction guide of consumer and corporate brands.

The emotional spark and authentic voice within every popular brand mimics human traits. Assigning human traits to corporate personalities by creative professionals kick-started the inevitable ascent of the personal brand movement.

Q: Why Create Your Brand?
A: You Are Selling. They are Buying.

The heart of a business may originate from laudable goals, like making a difference or changing the world, but the survival of a business requires customers. The agreement is simple: money in exchange for a product or a service. The same holds true for people and careers.

During business school, a marketing professor scolded our class for neglecting the last mile of job preparation. He suggested our logic and quantitative skills were substantial, yet we failed to package ourselves to attract employers. Students failed at the most basic tasks of communicating value and creating a human connection with the interviewer.

With this premise in mind, you are selling and employers are buying your services in the market exchange of work. You are an integrated product and services package available for hire in your chosen role and industry. You are the product manager of your own brand, responsible for design, development, pricing, and marketing.

Many consultants may object to the shameless art of sales and promotion as a reason to develop a personal brand. Yet everyone in the workforce is in sales, whether or not you claim to participate. For example, if you need approval for a department budget, you are in the business of selling and pitching your ideas. When you are competing for a job, you are selling the employer on why you are the best person for the role. Admit it, you are in sales!

You may have heard the question, "If a tree falls in the forest and no one is around to hear it, does it make a sound?" Being visible, having a voice, and communicating a clear message are essential brand activities. Your voice needs to be heard in the world of work. Getting out of the forest and developing your message are good places to start the brand building adventure.

Q: Why Maintain Your Personal Brand?
A: To Create a Sustainable Career Based on Trust

Zig Ziglar, the famed salesman, author, and motivational speaker, inspired the emotional bond of successful business relationships. This integral factor creates the foundation for the coveted playlist of brand ingredients.

> If people like you, they will listen to you. If they trust you, they will do business with you.
> —Zig Ziglar

Trust is a Vital Brand Element

Having worked in both sales and marketing, trust goals were easy to invoke as required essentials, yet often difficult to accomplish. I recently asked a friend of mine, Mark J. Carter, an entrepreneur and business development shaman, the reason for his successful event series on Idea Climbing™. Specifically, I wanted to know how he thoughtfully built his network, fostered awareness, and kindled business growth. His answer was to "embed yourself in the community and collaborate on a project." When I probed further, I observed his willingness to identify and collaborate on projects important to people in his network. He is in the business of helping people in his network to reach their goals.

Mark's behavior elicits trust, a catalyst for brand loyalty. Collaboration is at the heart of his personal brand values, creating an investment in his trust quotient with clients.

Now that we know why employees should create a personal brand, how do we get started? Let's peel back the layers of the process and walk through the steps. Then the fun part begins—analyzing a real person and her brand!

Personal Brand Development Model

Things are easier to remember when a mnemonic device is used, like a pattern of letters. If you like the letter D, I am Delighted, because each part of the process starts with D. The five steps are: Discover, Define, Design, Develop, and Deliver.

CAREER BRAND PROCESS

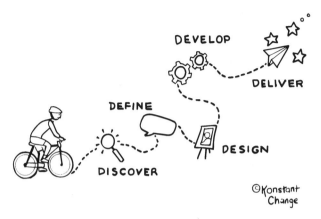

©Konstant Change

Discover

- Brand audit. How do you currently show up online? Do a Google search on your name. What content have you created in your career that is relevant and reusable for reinforcing your brand? Why do people work with you or seek you out in the workplace? Are you the go-to person for a particular set of skills?

- Brand exercises. Answer a series of questions to identify themes, interests, and patterns. Review content, images, people, and popular culture reflective of your personal style and preferences.

- Career insights. Identify behavior patterns and decisions regarding where and how you work.

- Self-awareness and analysis. Understand your strengths, influences, and guiding points of view. Answer these questions regarding your work and your environments: What do I like and what do I dislike? What am I better at than anyone else in my work environment?

- Career mapping. Sketch out your career journey, visually highlighting job roles and milestones. The visual depiction of progress or setbacks enables you to correlate patterns, strengths, and weaknesses uncovered in the brand exercises.

Define

- Brand position:
  Create a point of difference. Understand who you are, what you do, what industry you are in, and why anyone should care about you. This is your position statement.

- Brand values:
  These attributes communicate an attitude and the way you interact with people, investors, customers, or employers. They describe how people experience you. Brand values include a set of expectations and why you should be chosen over someone else for a job, an assignment, or board membership. These are words or phrases capable of summarizing who you are. Words like fearless, multidisciplined, or advocate, and phrases like "voice of reassurance" or "adjustments in real-time" are examples.

- Brand voice:
  If your brand were a person at a gathering, who would he be? The empathetic listener good friend, or like Sheldon Cooper from TV's *The Big Bang Theory*, who expounds about his vast knowledge regarding the universe? Should the tone of voice be aspirational or approachable?

Design

- Create a professional personal photo to be used across all digital platforms.

- Organize and manage phrases, words, and taglines that accompany your brand image.

- Create logos, icons, visual artifacts, illustrations, and photos associated with your personal brand to use in content like blog posts, marketing materials, articles, and websites.

- Develop resume formats, business cards, and a personal blog/website.

- Create brand standards or guidelines like color palette, photography style, and illustration approach.

Develop

- Create content for relevant social platforms: blog posts, LinkedIn updates, Twitter posts, Facebook posts, professional articles, SlideShare presentations, YouTube, and video content. The list is up to you.

- Develop assets for publishing online. Some popular places to store your content include Brandyourself.com and About.me. These personal branding sites are for individuals who do not want to create their own blog but would like to store their creative portfolio or writing samples. LinkedIn is another place to develop content. It is considered one of the most relevant places to store professional information.

Deliver

- Publish your material online on a regular basis and become a thought leader on the topics of interest and specialty.

- Spread your ideas via digital channels, in-person speaking engagements, and panel discussions.

- Test your messaging and brand story at networking events and during job interviews. Practice and repetition of key talking points will reinforce your unique brand.

- Interact with people on Facebook and within LinkedIn groups by commenting on interesting articles.

- That last presentation you made for your industry conference or article you published? Publish the presentation on SlideShare. Link to the article and the presentation via your LinkedIn profile. This business-to-business platform is a promotional billboard for your projects and accomplishments, not a redux of your resume. Give 'em your best shot as your profile picture.

• Become part of the evergreen fabric of the internet, where you and your ideas rise to the top.

Dare to Be Different

In the Definition phase of branding, you stake a claim on how you are different.

An enduring quote from a person who built a company based on her unique and memorable characteristics comes from a fashion icon:

> In order to be irreplaceable,
> one must always be different.
> —*Coco Chanel*

The Personal Brand Principle emboldens the agile careerist. My advice to job seekers and individuals who want to advance in their careers is: be bold and dare to be different. Coco's point of view further challenges us to forgo the axiom of replaceability on the path through our life's work.

Steve Jobs built the Apple dynasty and advertising campaign communicating, "Think Different." People who use Apple products identified with the strivers profiled in the campaign, like Gandhi, Eleanor Roosevelt, Muhammad Ali, Amelia Earhart, and John Lennon. Regardless of the millions of devices sold in a mass market, Apple users feel akin to the art of being different. They don't want to be like everyone else.

Different = memorable.

Personal Branding is a Deliberate Parallel Project

Let's review the process: Discover, Define, Design, Develop, and Deliver.

Whew! That's a lotta steps. However, you don't have to do it all at once. Similar to developing your skill sets through incremental education, the deliberate practice of defining Brand You is a career-enhancing project with predictable dividends.

Personal branding can be accomplished via a self-help workbook, online courses, workshops, or with the help of a brand coach. Think about this discipline as personal marketing.

With a self-directed attitude and patience of a methodical sculptor, you can be the architect of your own brand, one step at a time. Start working through the first few Ds as time permits. When the heavy lifting of the earlier stages is completed and momentum sets in, advance to the next stage of marketing you and your talents.

Remember, your brand is dynamic, rather than fixed. True to the inner workings of the agile careerist. Brand definition is subject to minor (or major) adjustments over the span of your life's work.

The Millennial Boost to Personal Branding

The Agile Careerist Project interviews with members of the millennial generation are lessons in personal definition. Taping and sharing videos from their phones, telling stories, writing blog posts, and documenting multiple facets of their lives is commonplace. What is most noticeable is their willingness to experiment with technology and push the limits of self-confidence. Millennials bring this same level of digital contribution to the workplace.

Other generations manifested youthful confidence in their twenties but did not possess the platforms to explore public expression and permanent footage during their invincible phases.

Millennial sharing habits are influenced by lifestyle and ideology.

The innovative generation is largely responsible for kicking the sharing economy into high gear, where access is more important than ownership. Companies like Airbnb and Uber epitomize this trend. While business model preferences differ from sharing online details, this generation has devised a comfort zone for the global exchange of ideas and information.

Self-expression is often a catalyst for self-awareness, step one in brand definition.

Personal Branding Instincts From Across the Pond

The youngest of three siblings, Katy Lynch moved from Scotland to the United States with her parents when she was twelve. Her sister, ten years older, influenced Katy regarding pop culture trends, international fashion, and creating a distinctive style. Katy was a sponge as she absorbed many insights and teen tips about personal brand awareness and definition.

Katy's reflections about coming of age on two continents invoked self-awareness terminology from the eyes of a twelve-year-old. She remembers gravitating toward "positive, uplifting, charismatic, think-outside-the-box people." Inspired by her brother's techie "leave no problem unsolved" cool factor, she adopted his friends, quickly discovering an inclination toward technical folk.

A self-described agile thinker, she rejected rigid environments, preferring the art of possibility surrounded by flexible, creative settings. She identified with her mother's artsy vitality, rather than her father's ultra-disciplined ways, a success requirement for his corporate job at a Fortune 100 company.

Katy made a decision in her early teens: she would never join the ranks of a large corporation. Her youthful assessment viewed big company employment as hampered by restrictions.

As a young immigrant from the United Kingdom, she forged her happiness by adapting to a country (the United States) with an oddly different sense of humor and pop culture trends. During this time, Katy honed her inquisitive nature and, in her words, "fiercely scrappy" and persistent demeanor.

One of her current mantras is "I get sh*t done." She has a determined streak, enabling her to solve her way out of formidable business challenges.

Entrepreneurial Verve and Genesis of a Leader

Despite her charming Scottish accent and long blonde curls, she is one feisty young millennial. Her unstoppable drive supports the persona of a badass businesswoman on the move. Her piercing blue eyes and serious gaze on her latest LinkedIn profile picture convey confidence with a no-nonsense attitude. You might even think it suggests a "don't mess with me" character.

As a savvy founder or cofounder of multiple startups, she can hold her own in a room full of customers, entrepreneurs, and investors. She's learned a few things about the dark side of entrepreneurship, yet preserves her positive values.

When Katy first moved to Chicago in 2008, she entered "startup jobs" in her Google search bar. Having worked a couple short stints for large companies in London and New York, she was clear that smaller and entrepreneurial were better aligned with her personality.

She landed at a startup called Where I've Been, a social networking application that marked its users' travel history on a color-coded map. There was no formal playbook for this emerging media channel, yet she created a social media instruction guide and adopted a test and measure mentality. The position as community manager included marketing, daily customer interaction, and hints of online support. The company attracted hundreds of thousands of users over a short period and was soon acquired by TripAdvisor.

When I first met Katy, she was the CEO of her social media business, SocialKaty, a company she launched in 2010. The firm was the first specialized agency in Chicago devoted entirely to social media marketing.

SocialKaty's niche evolved from figuring out how to talk to strangers on the internet to online community development for big brands. By the time she sold the company to Manifest Digital in 2014, the company had transformed into a brand research and consumer insights listening channel for large corporations. These major customers wanted to understand how online conversations impacted their own presence and marketplace value.

As an iterative, on-the-job learner, Katy's persona and actions illustrate personal brand building in action. Her early command of the social media communication style created a well-timed foundation for digital personal expression. Prior to social media, the possibilities or perils of personal marketing platforms did not exist.

In 2015, as CEO of TechWeek, the nation's largest traveling technology festival, Katy shone a spotlight on innovation while impressing observers with her technology chops. Through her role, she set an example for women in technology as they increasingly entered STEM (Science, Technology, Engineering, and Math) fields.

Heeding the entrepreneurial call yet again, she launched a new venture called Codeverse in 2017 with two partners, focused on the early education technology space. She and her partners created the first programming language designed specifically for kids and launched the world's first interactive coding studio.

Now that we've explored Katy's background and early influences, we are ready to see how she developed her personal brand platform.

Katy Gets Personal With Brand
The Brand Platform

With strong points of view about authentic communication, Katy Lynch subscribes to the merged personality philosophy of career brand management. She believes personal and business domains share a common, consistent personality.

To demonstrate how an individual creates and reflects her brand, let's unpack Katy's journey with a career map and illustrate the brand architecture elements of her journey. It starts early! We will frame it against the personal brand model steps mentioned earlier: Discover, Define, Design, Develop, and Deliver.

I offer you my deconstruction of Katy's brand elements, distilled from her career journey map, shown on the following page.

Case Study: Katy's Personal Brand Building Story Discover

Katy traversed between two continents at impressionable ages. She moved back to the United Kingdom for college and then to the United States once again, living in New York for a year before settling in Chicago. Her self-awareness was on high alert for many years as she figured out how to manage her individual rhythm of fitting in and standing out.

CAREER MAP

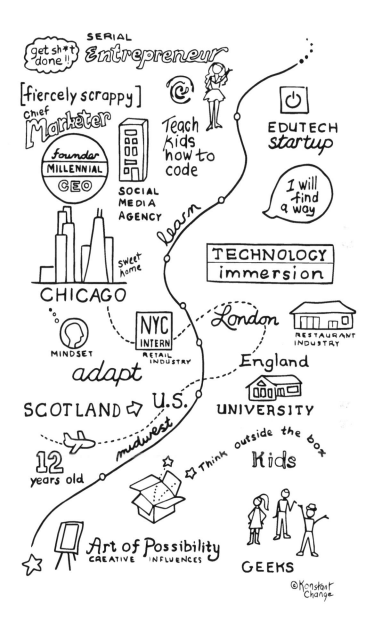

- Katy Lynch's brand chronicle started in the role of mentee, when her older sister coached her to cultivate a design and fashion sense. The self-expression exercises enabled Katy to reflect deeper than culture norms and establish a fundamental level of confidence.

- With a preference for positive people, she surrounded herself with uplifting and different mindset types of friends.

- She liked hanging out with her brother's cool friends, who exposed her to technology and the wonder of solving problems.

- The awkward entry as an immigrant at age twelve into the United States fostered an adaptive mentality and an independent streak.

- Artsy and agile triumphed over rigid and restrictive large corporate environments.

- Midwestern values and a feeling at home experience drew her to Chicago, where she expanded her roots.

- Her drivers are meeting new people and hearing new ideas.

- Picking apart ideas fuels her passion.

- Her "creator" community of people includes entrepreneurs, engineers, and venture capitalists.

- She immerses herself in a perpetual incubator of ideas.

- Craving disruption and first-mover advantage with new business ideas, she creates the rules in undefined territory. First mover describes people and companies who create and define new markets. These early movers often dominate the markets they create.

Define

As a deconstructive exercise in defining Katy's personal brand, I've outlined brand platform candidates for her position, values, and voice.

Brand Position:
Create a point of difference. Understand who you are, what you do, what industry you are in, and why anyone should care about you.

Position statement candidate for Katy: A fiercely scrappy innovator and serial entrepreneur who will pick apart an idea until it works for the market, is reworked, or rejected. Helps companies and investors vet promising ideas. A tastemaker.

Brand Values:
Values communicate an attitude and the way you interact with people, investors, customers, or employers. They describe how people experience you. Brand values include a set of expectations and why you are preferred over another. Values are a set of words or phrases summarizing who you are.

Katy's Value Candidates:
From the time she was a child, her imaginative style and questioning nature led to figuring it out. She works tirelessly to accomplish her work yet helps others to advance their ideas. Katy gets it done.

Inquisitive	Fiercely scrappy	Get sh*t done
I will figure out a way	Superhero	Advocate

Brand Voice:
Your voice is the tone and style in which you communicate. This is important in social media, where tone is experienced via snippets of thoughts, long-form content, video, and podcasts. What tone will attract your desired customers? If your brand were a person at a gathering, who would it be? The good friend who always has your back, like the characters of Harry Potter? Or Daenerys Targaryen, the Princess and Mother of Dragons from the series *Game of Thrones*? Her willful demeanor and visionary style enabled her to become a confident warrior woman. Should the tone of voice be aspirational or approachable? Funny or serious? Empathetic or authoritative? Educated or street smart?

Katy's Voice Candidates:
A determined entrepreneur advocate, helping people, sharing new ideas, and creating disruptive technology.

Determined	Helpful	Approachable
Passionate	Forward Thinking	Authentic

Design
Designed branding elements often include photos, illustration, and business cards. You can also start to use your brand definition in creative ways:

- With an integrated personal and business presence, Katy labeled her company with an elaboration of her own name, SocialKaty. Starting out as one person working out of her apartment and growing to twenty-five people in an office, she was the brand.

- SocialKaty's visual branding colors splashed vivid dark pink and black, expressing a confident attitude. Ninja characters complemented the personality of the firm. These brand characters were vigilant strategists making magic behind closed doors and throughout the social media sphere. Fun, yet productive.

- Her piercing blue eyes and serious gaze on her latest profile picture convey confidence with a no-nonsense attitude. A badass and "don't mess with me" attitude complement her likability. She is a young woman in command of who she is and what she wants to accomplish in life.

- Among other powerful young women, Katy was chosen for The Limited's The New Look of Leadership ad campaign. The look is serious and empowering, accomplished via fashionable contemporary clothing, and an intent no-smile photo that means business.

- She carries her technology analyst competencies and accents them with the packaging of an attractive fashionista. She sports bright colors, when appropriate (a way of standing out in business), while setting a serious tone with basic black. Oh, and she rocks the heels. All part of Katy's unique brand.

- There are three categories of interest via her self-described profile: entrepreneurship, marketing, and Chicago's tech scene.

- Among the categories that define Katy via her profile, she is an entrepreneur, investor, and superhero.

- As an inventive thinker and frequent communicator, she was named a Top 50 Tech Influencer by *Crain's Chicago* and was placed on Thrillist's Top 50 Twitter Feeds To Follow.

Develop

This step focuses on the practice of generating relevant content for people you want to attract or impress. By offering your point of view on specific topics, people will identify you with your preferred subject matter.

Content creation includes materials like speeches, presentations, blog posts, articles, infographics, and white papers. The good news is you may already be creating industry content via your existing job role. Content development is a critical part of keeping your information top of mind online. Personal blogs require a steady flow of fresh material. Other platforms like BrandYourself.com, Medium, About.me, and the LinkedIn network, based on broad communities, can be updated as often as desired.

- Katy crafts abundant presentations for speaking engagements on her chosen topics: entrepreneurship, marketing, and technology. Consistent content is a smart way to attract organizations looking for a speaker on these topics.

- She populated her LinkedIn profile, linking to relevant content published by her or written about her.

- With an eye on technology developments and trends, she weighs in and shares updates via social platforms, most notably Twitter, where she has over thirty thousand followers. She has earned thought leader status in the tech and marketing industries.

Deliver

With the content developed, it's time to create a schedule for posting content to various networks. You can monitor the networks and post comments to stimulate discussion on a particular topic. Some people create media calendars, while others post on an occasional basis.

- With her frequent and consistent social media posts and significant accomplishments, Katy now enjoys the benefit of publishers and journalists writing stories about her. She shares these ongoing articles with her network.

- Speaking engagements and workshops are a consistent opportunity for Katy to deliver valuable, relevant content.

- Comments and responses on social networks continue to reinforce Katy's brand.

Brand Platform Summary

With this brand framework, you can reference your brand guide as you communicate online or in person. You can make decisions based on your values and use a tone of voice consistent with your brand.

Like any worthy habit, consistency accompanies you on the path to becoming memorable.

PERSONAL BRANDING TOOLKIT

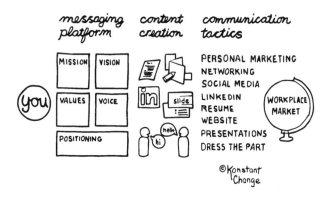

When researching this chapter, there were various articles about how to develop a personal brand, yet many of them focused on strategy and ignored the tactics. A DIY (do-it-yourself) summary of the process enables you to take charge of your own brand, with or without a coach. The goal of this exercise is to provide specific brand element examples to further the cause of your professional expression (and attraction!).

Let's take a closer look at the genesis of the personal branding movement. Movements develop in response to trends and challenges.

The Big Bang of the Personal Brand

The growth of personal branding materialized in response to two forces:

- Shrinking employment among conventional employers

- Rise of the "independent worker" movement

Corporate Employees

The crushing effects of the 2008 Global Financial Crisis altered the employee/employer agreement. Suddenly, talented employees struggled to protect their employment status. New college graduates joined the land grab of available jobs. The labor force participation rates were in free fall, and the luxury of career choice, based on passion, evaporated with the somber job reports. The new career playbook now required a chapter on why defining yourself in a unique way blasted beyond the velvet rope into the territory of steady employment.

Independent Workers

The number of entrepreneurs (some of them accidental) skyrocketed to fill the void of scarce work opportunities. This group contributed significantly to the growth of the solopreneur and free agent movements. We now have phrases to describe these behaviors: the freelance economy and gig economy. Oh, and these phrases are in good company with the on-demand economy. According to a survey by MBO Partners, there are nearly eighteen million solopreneurs in the United States and an additional twelve million independent workers who hold side gigs.

The survey definition of an independent worker is: anyone over age twenty-one with a job status as independent consultant/contractor, self-employed worker, freelance worker, temporary worker, fixed-term contract worker, on-call worker or small business owner with fewer than four employees.

This resourceful group of individuals required a boost of unique expression to attract customers.

Having Your Say

Corporate employees, solopreneurs, and independent workers traveled the road of differentiation to attract available work. They applied personal branding tactics for employment preservation, job-seeking activities, and customer attraction.

The troubled economy created a breeding ground for career pivot points, altering the future of work by changing the value equation between employer and employee. A compressed job market inspired an innovative spirit among job seekers and entrepreneurs, who learned and invented the basics of personal brand development. The earliest adopters were the new millennials entering the workforce in 2009.

Prior to the Big Bang of personal branding, the personal value rules existed within a different set of rules and agents. Employment agencies, job boards, business cards, and resumes once dominated the practice of representation governing the supply and demand for employment. Employer reviews had the final say on individual value in our profession.

The storms of change and financial disruption have incited the dawn of self-direction and personal definition. Just like the '60s, an age of intense individual discovery, every new generation goes through the coming of age questions of "Who am I?" and "What is my purpose?"

Global workers no longer have the luxury of considering this a phase. As Gary Lew, a writer, entrepreneur, and historian, states, "This is your world. Shape it or someone else will." While Gary was referring to the entire world, the quote is highly relevant for branding.

Lucky for us, we get to choose how we show up. Having your say means you can shape perception about you like never before.

Sustainable State of Personal Branding

The career-branding phenomenon is here to stay. It is a burgeoning industry, with an ecosystem of software vendors, assessment tools, branding platforms, coaches, website developers, designers, writers, branding firms, and a vast assortment of consultants.

Three compelling motivational quotes, reflective of brand, caught my attention. These thoughts underline compelling reasons for defining you.

Law of Attraction
> Knowing where you're going is irresistibly attractive.
> —*Liz Strauss, entrepreneur, author, speaker, marketer,*
> *social media influencer, and retreat producer*

Differentiation
> There has never been and never will be another you. You have a purpose—a very special gift that only you can bring to the world.
> —*Marie Forleo, life/business coach, motivational speaker,*
> *author, and founder of online B-School and* MarieTV

Be Memorable
> I don't do average. I do unforgettable.
> —*Michelle Ruiz, broadcast journalist, entrepreneur,*
> *speaker, and former Los Angeles news anchor*

The word "brand" is not contained in the quotes, yet these passages validate the importance of claiming a distinctive place on the planet of your life's work.

A Story of Brand Values

During a conversation with Liz Strauss, a business coach and a perceptive people observer, the deeper meaning of personal brand simmered to the surface. Her career path included teacher, sales professional, international publishing editor, business strategist, conference producer, and author, among others.

While Liz accomplished notable milestones, like leading a strategy turnaround for a troubled publisher, one pervasive characteristic captures her genius talent: her thoughtful teacher intellect motivates people to examine and change their lives.

Liz is a brain picker who exemplifies what it means to be different. Tall and lean, with wispy blonde chin-length hair, her commanding presence is felt through silent pauses, as much as her pondering words. Her serious blue eyes, especially when she sets her bent index finger beneath her chin, communicate in a direct, concise manner. She speaks in pithy, quotable sound bites, especially when the social expectations of small talk escape her rational brain.

Via Twitter, one of the first early wildfire social platforms, she established a strategy for substantial online conversations, 140 characters at a time. She was one of the first non-celebrity bloggers, via her Successful Blog website, to attract thousands of followers, offering wisdom about business, life, music, and writing. Her ascent to attracting one hundred thousand followers on Twitter was swift. As she describes the attributes of her personal style, she defines it as sensitive; I see it as also empathetic.

Like the journey to the depths of the ocean containing an expansive masterpiece of activity and beauty, Liz probes beneath the surface. She accomplishes this by posing questions and by challenging the way things have been done in the past. This was on full display via her conferences, SOBCON and Genius Shared. Her educational format inspires people to create what's possible for them, via a mastermind format.

Liz Strauss's gift of understanding herself enables her to fully define her characteristics in a consistent and direct manner. In our conversations, her conferences, and her latest book, *Anything You Put Your Mind To*, there are three recurring personal brand themes:

- Change your mind (the stories you believe) and you can change your life.
- Make all decisions based on your values.
- You can do it; recognize the brilliance in you.

When I asked Liz to describe her values, her immediate response startled me. Most people are not able to repeat the attributes guiding their lives. Her values are evergreen. Consistent over a period of many years, they are:

- Trust
- Loyalty
- Ability to make a decision
- Sense of place
- Ability to see beauty and wonder

After reading her latest book, her "ability to see beauty and wonder" value is displayed in Technicolor. People who know Liz would agree these values summarize her. What are your brand values?

As previously stated in the chapter, your brand development process can be broken down into steps over a length of time. Your discovery process may be less intense than others; your brand values may be immediately apparent. Like a researcher establishing a hypothesis, you may generate a list of values that are subject to the repeated question, "Is this me?"

Wisdom of Alignment

Pondering Liz's curious choice of the brand value "ability to make a decision," her uncanny self-awareness and fierce commitment to moving forward are evident. To their detriment, many organizations do not prioritize decision making as a key value. Early on in the discovery process, corporate leaders often insist on values like innovative, excellence, or integrity. They soon recognize the sameness of their words, and dig much deeper to uncover what makes them different.

"Ability to make a decision" is an undisputed winner of practical progression.

As Liz mentioned, "Any time you make a decision, you can ask yourself, are you in alignment with your values?" If the answer is no, it's time to rethink your decision or reframe the problem. Her value sits at the convergence of alignment and growth, a position of strength for the career traveler.

Think Different

When interviewing for a job, there are typically a number of candidates vying for the same role. The scene is similar to an audition for an acting role, where you must answer the question "Why should we hire you?" Many people have comparable qualifications, yet you must distinguish yourself by sharing a unique story or creating a memorable experience.

During business school I interviewed for a highly competitive internship with Apple. I thought, how can I "Think different." like the company's famous slogan? The interview was positive, yet more was needed to differentiate me from the other candidates. I created a small storybook as a follow-up package. The clever storytelling documented a buyer's journey as she shopped for her computer. The book included photos of me engaging with retail clerks and personal user reviews of several Macs. I received an offer the day after delivering the books to the front desk.

You are the most valuable asset of your career journey. Just as startups and companies require marketing investment to stand out in a crowded arena, your value needs to be defined and promoted to gain attention in the workplace.

Having a clear set of brand themes and values simplifies the decision-making process on the path of your life's work. Your brand platform allows you to develop messaging, speak your truth, and respond in a consistent and reliable manner. Fellow workers, friends, and colleagues know what to expect and come to rely on your consistency.

You will benefit from uncovering and defining your remarkable value in the noisy marketplace of work opportunities. Your clear voice will rise above the chatter and common jargon of the undifferentiated employee.

In summary, the branding process will help you answer the questions:

- Who are you?
- What makes you special?
- Why should anyone care?

Concise responses to these questions will open the secret doors to earned confidence and professional possibilities.

C'mon, hop on the branding bus and get started with the next phase of your meaningful career. All of the cool kids are on board!

As you will see in the next section, the more the merrier when it comes to connecting career branding efforts with business branding practices in the workplace. You will learn how the laws of attraction and amplification apply to you, your employer, or your entrepreneurial business.

Dating Advice: For Personal, Employer, and Corporate Brands
Better together. Yep, just like collaborative teams yield a more
noticeable and timely result than one person working solo.
Similarly, a significant personal brand increases in value when
combined with employer or corporate brands. Conversely,
employer and corporate brands expand their worth when
integrated with smart personal brands.

The advice is to harmonize branding efforts for greater
impact. The attraction between individual and corporate
brands forms a productive bond yielding mutual benefits.

Using marketing programs as an example, it has long been
known three or more marketing campaign tactics work
better than just one. This approach is referred to as integrated marketing and creates better results for companies
than isolated tactics, like advertising, email, or public relations. The reason is each activity, working in concert with
one another, amplifies the results of a related activity. The
return on investment (ROI) is greater than when activities
are launched as solo efforts. An integrated campaign with
optimal timing achieves exponential results.

The marketing analogy is effective because branding is a
marketing tactic. Let's take a closer look at the relationship
between the three types of branding in the workplace:

- Personal branding = marketing and positioning
  of you.

- Employer branding = marketing and positioning
  of a company to a specific group of people for
  the purpose of attracting and retaining talent:
  potential or existing employees.

- Corporate branding = marketing and positioning
  of a company to a broad group of stakeholders:

potential/current customers, investors, media, business partners, and employees.

The Way We Were

Up until recently, corporate branding, employer branding, and personal branding were siloed operations. Many employers viewed personal branding with suspicious eyes. The company point of view was further complicated by trust and loyalty issues. After all, employers were more interested in employee value within their organization, rather than individual value on the open or external market.

A high-potential employee could quickly become a departure threat as her star rose and she became more valuable in a particular industry. An employee groomed by one company could become attractive to a competing company with an enticing offer. The balance between positive reinforcement and keeping significant contribution under wraps created tension and mixed signals.

My Aunt Cele, a food chemist, once received a substantial check from her employer for a whipped topping patent created while she was employed there. She received the bonus with the stipulation her financial compensation be hidden from her fellow employees and industry players. While the patent was public, the secrecy of the reward kept her economic acknowledgement private. Positive reinforcement accompanied by a gag order.

Before the employer-employee contract changed, freelance endeavors were forbidden. Side gigs, an expression of an individual brand, were viewed as a betrayal of company loyalty.

Companies focused on their own brands, rather than encouraging individual brands. This is still true in many businesses today, but is changing rapidly to conform to the evolution of the work environment.

When I was a graphic designer for an advertising agency, I hid my freelance activity from my employer. Contrast that to recent years, where I advised startups, delivered marketing strategy solutions, and produced industry events in parallel with my executive responsibilities.

The world of work is changing; adapt or get left behind. The repetitive advice is relevant for corporations and individuals. The free agent economy, reliant on knowledge exchange among the three branding entities, forms a synchronous relationship.

Let's see how the interlocking gears of businesses, individuals, and information create a compelling brand equation.

How Can We All Work Together?

Depending on your perspective, there are different goals with three seemingly different agendas:

- Personal branding: differentiate individuals.

- Employer branding: attract and retain best available talent.

- Corporate branding: build and reinforce value of company in minds of customers, stockholders, and other stakeholders.

Yet there are unmistakable benefits for companies who embrace personal brand champions among their ranks. Formerly perceived as threats, career branding habits and actions by employees are transformed into opportunities for companies. Following are a few examples:

The Corporate Advocate
A worker who speaks on behalf of his company at an industry conference initiates a set of complementary branding results.

He reinforces his business expertise across a broad group of industry participants, increasing his value as a thought leader. He also expands positive company awareness, strengthens the corporate brand, and attracts potential employees who may be in the audience. A solid win for all three types of branding.

Knowledge gained by attending and speaking at a conference, for example, will be shared with colleagues and team members—yet another corporate benefit. Trends and industry breakthroughs discovered at these gatherings offer new perspectives and serve to stimulate corporate innovation. Innovative ideas and fresh thinking are impressive returns on professional development when it is seasoned with the bonus of personal brand activities.

Social Skills

Today's job candidates are rigorous researchers, an important trend impacting employer brands. Job seekers have access to the largest database of online information via their browser when vetting a potential employer. Companies that support and encourage personal brand activities via social media will reap the rewards of positive searchable content about their businesses.

A satisfied employee who affiliates with his company across social platforms like LinkedIn or Twitter expands positive exposure for the business enterprise. Discoverable through online search, comments provided on LinkedIn or tweets tying industry information to companies stimulate conversation and awareness. These accessible forms of content contribute to informative nuggets in the job search universe.

With curiosity and preparation as their guides, job candidates often reach out and connect with existing employees of their target employer within their LinkedIn network. They pursue further exploration of the company through phone calls and in-person meetings.

Personal branding is the ally of professional and personal development. Leaders in organizations who endorse this practice inside their doors are better equipped to manage the flow of constructive information about their company. Supportive employee development behavior inspires positive comments on sites like Glassdoor, a company review site.

The potential dark side of company affiliation via online sites is workers will express their satisfaction AND unhappiness on employer review sites. Forward-thinking employers will consider two things: acceptance of employee expression and training on personal branding practices. Better to invest in personal brand development workshops for their employees who will see it as a perk than risk the downside of disgruntled online comments. These activities will mitigate the effect of an occasional discontented online remark.

One of the immediate internal benefits of personal branding within a company is you can better understand the capabilities of workers across an organization. Wouldn't it be great to have a database of employees sorted by their succinct offerings and position statements? When you have a need for a program, you could request a team member for a project based on what the individual cares about, rather than referencing a job description or list of skill sets.

The Personal Publisher

Employees are prolific publishers of content like speeches, industry blog posts, white papers, technical briefs, presentations, and videos. Much of this content is produced in alliance with corporate or product marketing departments, yet the author signature is a display of the personal brand. Personal brand awareness is transparently integrated with corporate and employer brands.

For example, a well-written white paper or a speech with significant industry reach will bode well for the individual and the company. Businesses who inspire personal brand building by encouraging creation of useful industry content by employees will fortify their market awareness. They will also recruit top job candidates who uncover employee-generated content while conducting research.

Some employees develop their own unbranded (no reference to their company within the post) industry content, profiling their expertise on a specific topic. Connection with a company on these posts via the biography will enhance corporate presence by association with a talented author. Examples are trade publication articles and blog posts within the vast network of industry bloggers.

Publishing platforms like personal blogs, individual branding sites, LinkedIn, and Medium offer fertile ground for new ideas, opinions, how-to articles, and industry information. For example, LinkedIn is the default personal business platform for individuals. Presentations on SlideShare, articles, research results, news coverage, and commentaries are highlighted within the platform. Much of the content is industry-specific, such as the output from a conference presentation, and is branded with corporate logos on SlideShare or YouTube videos.

Some of the content may be colocated on company and industry sites or exist as links to another site. A meaningful insight is employees taking pride in the work they accomplish at their company by sharing it to the public (non-proprietary, of course!).

The digital footprint is the first impression between job candidates and people working within the company. The 24/7 content serves as a prelude to the first handshake or direct eye contact in the talent recruitment pipeline.

Biographies as lead magnets and branded megaphones

When I worked as a brand strategist for global law firm clients, there was an obsessive focus on website information by partners within the firm. Within one firm, the expertise of 1,200 partners in one hundred countries, nine industries, and fifteen practice areas was critical to the success of the corporate brand.

We learned the most powerful marketing content on many professional services firms' websites was the partner biography section. The data analytics indicated users spent most of their time in this area, rather than the home page or the "about" section.

People and companies hire lawyers, not just law firms. This was my first indoctrination into the brand value of precise individuals within firms. No surprise: some partners were in higher demand than others.

Leadership Branding

The leaders in the C-suite bear a similar responsibility to corporate and employer brands. The burden of correct commentary and appropriate responses is significant. Online access by customers and investors to videos, speeches, and quotes in the media represent influential data points for a company brand.

Media training and coaching are essential parts of brand management for executives. A CEO's personal brand and her public interaction with customers is an extension of the corporate public persona.

Personal Brands and Talent Recruitment

Recruiters, hiring managers, and human resource leaders look for culture fit and online social footprint, along with the many skill requirements necessary to fulfill a particular position. As they sift through the vast mountain of applicants, the standouts rise to the top because of aligned personal brand definition. Hiring decision makers apply the company brand filter as a vetting tool for choice.

A job seeker will create a noticeable advantage by crafting a digital story in advance of the candidate selection process.

When a candidate conducts his own Google search, what results are on the first page? Does his LinkedIn profile contain sufficient activity and content applicable to the company or industry? Are his brand personality and communication style a good fit for the company? For example, a person who blogs about industry issues relevant to his target company will attract the attention of recruiters and hiring managers.

Matches are made when commonalities exist after passing through the gauntlet of good-fit filters.

The best part comes next! Real people who handle branding integration like champs. We will profile examples of how personal branding dovetails with corporate and employer branding.

Three-Part Harmony with Personal, Corporate, and Employer Brands

Personal brand all-stars in the business world are visible within an industry or among the general public. These clever communicators are consummate brand ambassadors for employers. They possess three traits:

1. A natural flair for promotion with a purpose

2. Wise alignment of published content with key industry and enterprise messages

3. Unmistakable passion for their craft

As a personal branding analyst, I've identified a few careerists who have mastered brand integration by courting their respective markets with dexterity and ease.

World-class Brand Champion: Richard Branson

As a leader of more than four hundred companies within Virgin Group, Richard Branson's brand is synonymous with:

- Multipreneurism
- Humanitarian instincts
- Anything is possible
- Taking risks
- Persistence
- Solving burning problems
- Thinking big

Branson's genius is visible via his devout interaction with the entrepreneur community. He holds contests and publishes articles in countless publications devoured by readers who want to understand how to work, create, and be successful entrepreneurs.

His speeches on risk taking and failure are classic lessons for people and companies who want to grow. As founder and motivational leader at Virgin, he is the flag-carrying champion of the company.

Remember his attempted balloon trip across the Pacific in 1991? Instead of Los Angeles, he landed in the Artic but almost crashed into the ocean. The edgy adventure is a stunning example of risk taking in action and 100 percent consistent with his brand. From record labels to airlines, Richard Branson is a founder who publishes, speaks, and acts in support of the Virgin brand.

Branson's antics and activities attract employees who relate to his sense of adventure and embrace a persistent work ethic. The company is known for revamping current business models that address consumer needs; Virgin Airlines's customer-centric treatment of passengers is a perfect example. The corporate brand is rewarded with happy repeat buyers, consistent profits, and a steady flow of business and investors.

You may be thinking, we can't all be like a world-renowned entrepreneur! I started with Richard Branson as an example because high-profile personalities make quick, digestible case studies. The rest of the examples are real-people careerists. I promise!

The Transfer Effect: David Armano

In 2009, on the eve of the lightning-fast spread of the social media movement within the digital marketing landscape, David Armano joined the next wave of online interaction. Already a seasoned creative agency leader, he was known in the creative industry as a thought leader for visual thinking, marketing strategy, and brand development. He created programs for Estee Lauder, P&G, Adidas, United Airlines, Taco Bell, HP, and Bally Total Fitness, among others.

David joined Edelman, the world's largest independently owned public relations firm, as one of the company's first social media hires, overseeing a complete revamp of Edelman.com. He grew the firm's Twitter following to over fifty thousand while collaborating with the digital chair to develop the social business practice, now 20 percent of the agency's revenues.

Which brings us to the positive impact of David's personal brand on the Edelman brand. His personal organic following across social channels exceeds eighty-five thousand. His widely read personal blog, *Logic+Emotion*, covers brand strategy, marketing, and the business of the social web. He has spoken at venues like TEDx, SXSW, Forrester, Microsoft, O'Reilly, and Google. His articles are featured on *Harvard Business Review, Forbes,* and *Fast Company*.

David represents topics germane to Edelman's core business, enabling him to attract and close new business. Many companies are exposed to the Edelman brand through his keynote speeches and articles. Prospective employees, who know David in the Twittersphere as @armano, trust him, a feeling that transfers to the Edelman brand.

The Long Game Endowment Brand: Scott Malpass

In 1989, when Scott Malpass was just twenty-six years old, he took over the chief investment officer position for the University of Notre Dame. Since that time, he built the endowment from $453 million to over $10 billion. He is considered to have one of the top track records in the endowment management business. The university's endowment value is in the top ten nationwide.

Scott's view of the long game earned him a nickname. Michael Moritz, a partner at venture capital firm Sequoia Capital in Menlo Park, California, referred to him as the Warren Buffet of the endowment arena.

As Malpass developed the Notre Dame model for investing (in contrast to the Harvard and Yale models), he heightened the university's investor brand. He also expanded the school's ability to provide scholarships. With two degrees from Notre Dame, including an MBA, Scott's untarnished record of performance elevated his personal brand in the investment industry.

He is a sought-after speaker, author of many articles, member of numerous boards, and recipient of multiple industry awards, including a Lifetime Achievement Award by CIO Magazine. As a director or advisory council member for a variety of investment and charitable organizations, Scott extends his talent to help other worthy institutions. A recent appointment included the chair of the board of directors for TIFF Advisory Services (TAS), where more than seven hundred US nonprofits manage about $9.5 billion in assets. And late last year, he was named a member of the board of the Vatican Bank.

Scott Malpass, admired by young students and business professionals alike, magnifies the glow of the Notre Dame employer brand. The relationship between Scott's personal brand and the University of Notre Dame's brand is long term, just like his approach to investing.

Crafting a Good Life: Jonathan Fields

Jonathan Fields's insights into living a good life stem from his experiences, a number of *Good Life Project* interview recordings (audio and video), and conversations. He ends each interview with one question: What does it mean to live a good life? The rich responses from business leaders, artists, and entrepreneurs are profound and inspiring.

Similar to Simon Sinek's association with the question Why? or Oprah Winfrey's connection with possibility, Jonathan's brand and priorities are akin to a good life.

Growing up between the disciplines of creative expression via his mother/artist and the study of cognitive science through his professor/researcher father, Jonathan Fields developed a unique sense of life's possibilities.

After launching side businesses in his youth and during college, Jonathan took a self-proclaimed career detour as a hedge fund and securities lawyer. Within a few years, the long hours and stress of misaligned values and personal expression led him to choose an entrepreneurial path based on purpose and balance.

The course correction story validates his brand and the ability we all have to make changes on the path to a more mindful life.

Although he built multiple businesses, including a series of yoga studios, he is most known for his work on the Good Life Project, www.goodlifeproject.com, an education and media company. The company provides experiences and training to cultivate more "meaningful, connected, and vital lives." I participated in one of his Entrepreneurial Alignment Labs to further my ideas and obtain feedback for the Agile Careerist Project.

He is the author of three books that transport readers through life's essential questions regarding careers, uncertainty, and what it means to live a good life.

In his book, How to Live a Good Life, he illustrates his three-bucket equation for sustaining a balanced life:

- Vitality: Optimize state of mind and state of body.

- Connection: Build deep, meaningful relationships on multiple levels.

- Contribution: Bring to the world your gifts that align with who you are.

He also shared the following values during our interview: work with and serve people you love, inspire possibilities for others, pursue perpetual learning, be creative, and be a maker. A discerning list of priorities.

The Good Life Project corporate brand and Jonathan's personal brand are in 100 percent alignment!

The Future of Personal Branding

Imagine walking down a busy street or a hustling city center filled with colors, textures, shapes, and a dissonant collection of noises. In the United States, Times Square in New York comes to mind. The signs flash with pictures and words, cars stuck in traffic jams sound their boisterous horns, and a pedestrian frantically waves his arm and yells, "Taxi!" Street performers compel us to take notice, and street vendors selling fruit and magazines capture a tiny portion of our available attention. Noise and visual stimulation envelop us on the way to work. It seems everyone is on a mission or heading to an important meeting in places like Times Square.

The Times Square analogy is the information overload we experience every day in our workplace, where numerous agendas compete for our attention. Add a few trips to the airport and rides on various forms of public transportation to mimic the perpetual movement of our work existence. The tiny computer (um, phone) in our pocket vibrates, alerting us about the greatest interrupter in our lives, the urgent text.

How do you stand out among the relentless blitz of technology, roaring noise, and insistent change?

Personal branding, the antidote to running with the undifferentiated pack of people at work, will help you get noticed in the sea of career sameness. Like Marie Kondo, the Japanese cleaning consultant and best-selling author who demonstrated the "life-changing magic of tidying up," you can sort through the clutter of your life's work.

Understanding who you are, how you are different, and how to communicate this to potential employers and people within your current organization will inspire confidence. Rock solid foundation for staying above the fray. The reputation meter starts ticking the minute you enter the workplace, yet you can take steps at any point to create and shape your values and genuine career contribution.

The personal branding phenomena will continue to grow in importance as a strategy for owning creativity, growth, and happiness throughout your career.

The next time you experience the disorienting encounter of being caught in a metaphorical Times Square of noise, take a deep breath. You have the tools to declutter the landscape by defining and claiming a unique position in the workplace.

Next Steps

There are five steps in the personal brand building process:

- Discover
- Define
- Design
- Develop
- Deliver

Getting started is often the hardest part. Yet personal brand exercises are engaging and rewarding because they are all about you.

To understand your professional value and personal branding point of difference, review the following list of tactics within the numbered steps. Start your personal branding process by picking two tactics within one of the steps. Create a document and get feedback from a mentor or a trusted friend.

Ready? Let's launch your confidence-boosting exercises!

1. Discover. Gather insights from your network regarding your strengths, traits, or capabilities.

   - Send out individual emails (do NOT send out a broadcast request) to a trusted group of family members, friends, and work buddies. Pose the question, "What adjectives come to mind regarding my strengths, traits, or capabilities?" or "What do you think are my strong suits?"

   - Complete the following sentence: "I am better than anyone else when it comes to _____." Elaborate on more than one.

2. Define. Create a position statement.

   - Recall defining moments in your life. Create a list of unique personal characteristics you know to be true as a result of these milestones or setbacks.

   - Create a test position statement that includes the following content: who you are, what you do, your area of work or specialty, and why anyone should care. Example for a product manager: As an inventive product manager for the technology software industry, I integrate the voice of the customer, product packaging skills, and pricing strategy to meet revenue forecasts. My street-smart market savvy, sense of humor, and approachable demeanor position me as a trusted advisor within the company, helping me to lead and inspire performance among teams. I am the go-to person when it comes to turning around or rescuing a challenging product launch.

Extra Credit

- Take the Strengths test provided by Gallup, an automated online measurement tool for defining your strengths. Here is the link: https://www.gallup-strengthscenter.com/Purchase/en-US/Product

  It takes fifteen minutes to answer a few questions. You will receive an automated strengths summary. Review the copy and evaluate whether the assessment is on target. If so, test some phrases for relevance to include in your values list, position statement, or promotional copy.

- Do a competitive LinkedIn review of people in your profession or related line of business. Update your summary section in the first person so this section reads as a billboard for who you are and what you are looking for. This section is not intended to be a bullet list of what is on your resume.

- Update the heading next to your picture on your LinkedIn profile to reflect a functional description of your talents that is keyword searchable by corporate recruiting bots. An example is educational technologist, rather than simply educator.

CHAPTER 7

Principle Six: Activate the Feedback Squad

We all need people who will give us feedback. That's how we improve.
—BILL GATES

Hard Work, the Prequel to Feedback

In the Midwest, wide-open spaces and rustling golden prairies dominated the pre-suburbia landscape of my childhood. The genesis of industrious inspiration started with the inclement, blustery weather of the plains and landed on poet Carl Sandburg's shoulders. He colored Chicago with the phrase, "Stormy, husky, brawling, City of the Big Shoulders . . ." suggestive of an unstoppable energy and collective strong work ethic.

Carl Sandburg understood the blue-collar roots of the urban streets and instilled the satisfaction derived from a day's work. Yet in the universe of career advances, working hard is not enough.

My youthful indiscretion was thinking I could go it alone.

The test track for job strategies was not included on any school syllabus. The best preparation by a rookie for a first job involved showing up and buckling up for the unpredictable ride.

Oh, and adopt the work ethic christened in Carl Sandburg's poem.

Working harder than anyone else guaranteed a rewarding ascent to the summit of my dreams, or so I thought. Fiendishly racking up the hours of work, with a heads-down mentality, I believed rewards correlated to level of effort. My first boss fed the myth by admonishing his team to prove their worth via the sweat of weekend hours.

Principle Six: Activate the Feedback Squad

While perspiration and hard work bookend the career design formula, my naïve assessment of the work puzzle ignored coworkers, workplace politics, and "in your corner" advocates. You can't be a trailblazer without help.

Let's discuss the principle.

Activate the Feedback Squad Principle

No one can do it alone. Seek the advice of people you respect: mentors, trusted friends, and savvy colleagues. You can also pay it forward by participating in a feedback squad for others through mentorship or conversational guidance.

Activating the feedback squad principle is a resounding ode to the inner circle, the leaders, and booster club members of your career team. Their generous guidance, honest feedback, and "I believe in you" sound-bites inspire a pattern of confidence and good decisions.

Sounds logical, right? Yet many of us prefer to make our professional mistakes in shamed silence, rather than ask for help. The habit of seeking feedback must be learned and nurtured to benefit our career aspirations. The ultimate ask is a humble yet powerful action.

This chapter will:

- Explain the value of advice and feedback.

- Help you identify potential mentors and workplace advocates.

- Outline various types of career feedback: mentorship, peer advice, leadership, friends, family.

- Profile examples of agile careerists who cultivate the habit of seeking and applying feedback to enhance their careers.

- Illustrate how to engage in a feedback loop.

Baseline: The Age of Inexperience

In the age of inexperience, prior to learning how to work and before imagining the perfect job, we absorbed the world around us through a steady fire hose of fresh ideas. Ushering in the era of preference, we chose options along the shores of grand possibility. We accumulated abundant experiences while shaping carefully crafted attitudes about our life's work.

In my own experience, the gradual waves of decision points and active blending of knowledge prompted my occupational roles of choice. While learning about work, however, the struggle to find the missing manual and the personal performance coach who had my back loomed large.

Alter Your Feedback Reality

With requisite formal training, amplified by teacher input, we entered the career stage alone. Many of us went out on a limb, the branch bending with the weight of limited experience. The elusive career mentorship invitation, reserved for the chosen few, never arrived.

The feeling of being left out is valid. Over 80 percent of people interviewed for this book confessed they had no official mentor throughout their career. You may recognize the executive advocate, missing in action for most of us. Picture the well-connected senior leader, approximately ten to fifteen years older (and wiser), meeting with you frequently to ensure workplace success. Yeah, that one.

Despite the lack of designated influential leaders in their lives, many of these workers made significant advances in the workplace. Upon studied reflection, they were not truly alone. They received feedback from trusted advisors at regular intervals and at key inflection points.

As a member of the 80 percent club, lacking a long-term traditional wise mentor, composing this chapter exposed an annoying vulnerability. The nagging feeling I had missed the rite of passage for workplace potential, as defined by higher powers. The disturbing awareness left me at odds with my past. It was as if the game of business was played on the golf course, and I lacked the training and experience to compete.

However, meeting other successful people who shared a similar experience enabled me to reconcile three profound truths:

- A feedback loop is self-directed and accessible by all workers.

- The definition of mentors and mentorship expands beyond the senior leader advocate, including a vast assortment of friends, colleagues, and trusted advisors.

- Being authentic to who you are will attract your tribe of helpers. Maybe you run triathlons instead of playing golf.

Discussing this topic with talented careerists minimized the memories of my insecurities and reminded me of my unique strengths. I also realized personal accountability is a muscle that must be exercised.

The limited definition of a traditional mentor requires a reboot. The casting call for feedback is open for supportive people already in your orbit. A reflective acknowledgement of trusted advisors and influencers on your career timeline will help to better identify members of your feedback team.

The Habits of Feedback Seekers

The difference between those who are in command of their professional journey and those who flounder in the abyss of career envy lies in three areas:

1. Accountability

2. Feedback team

3. Persistent performance improvement

Accountability

The era of reliance on human resources departments and bosses to help manage your career has migrated to the waveforce of self-direction. Some bosses may turn into vibrant and vocal advocates, while others simply expect you to accomplish your work with a low-maintenance demeanor. As the CEO of your career, you are the insightful champion for your growth, capably surrounding yourself with proper people resources and feedback for directing your life's work.

Feedback Team

Trustworthy feedback enables personal growth and improved performance—valuable elements of career success. You may remember one particular mentor, or a series of people who cared about your development. Your brain trust of feedback advocates are similar to a treasured collection of souvenirs, evoking memories of your experiences, yet fostering future dreams.

Posing the question "How can I be better?" launches a feedback squad worthy of your cultivation.

Persistent Performance Improvement

Like mastery of skills, the quest for career finesse is derived from frequent practice, timely coaching comments, and a willingness to fine tune your actions. A tenacious work ethic and humble openness to constructive critique will lead to improved performance in your career trek.

Working hard is a brilliant foundation for accomplishment, yet the percussive beat of growth lies in improvement.

The great thing about the habits of feedback seekers is they can be adopted and learned.

With a seat in the power position of feedback awareness, you will gain access to nuggets of wisdom and guidance. Like the virtual reality headsets required for seeing multiple dimensions of designed habitats, your feedback goggles will manifest advisors in your career environment.

The Feedback Whisperer

Across the uneven terrain of business, Ann Hoeger is a gale force wind of movement with the precision skills of a Swiss watchmaker. Her uncanny human nature barometer separates the players from the posers, a convenient skill when assembling or joining teams.

Ten years ago, while attending a networking event of strangers, I noticed Ann's sly smile and quick assessment maneuvers in a crowded room. Her shoulder-length wavy hair complemented her black St. John knit suit. As an arbiter of good taste, she personified "dress for success."

She asked more questions than she spoke about herself. If I had been pressed for three words to describe Ann, my first impressions were: consummate professional, design thinker, and charismatic. This is her story.

Grounded in engineering and operations management, Ann evolved into the roles of consumer goods brand strategy, VP of marketing, and innovation consultant. The varied progression reflects her continuous learning appetite.

From curiosity about how things work to observing behavior patterns of consumers, she is a feedback whisperer. Her accessible presence and ability to gain trust in conversation serve as a catalyst for critique.

When I asked Ann about mentors in her career, she did not cite any one individual. She actively seeks out feedback and support from a broad variety of people. In Ann's world, mentors are organized in the following categories:

- Senior management, where she discusses business systems, leadership, and how to navigate the corporate landscape. These relationships helped her develop a deep competence in organizational strategy.

- Younger workers, where Ann welcomes reverse mentoring relationships. Keeping up with new trends and essential skills are top priorities. Ann derives career currency by staying current.

- Peer groups, a safe harbor for addressing challenges, sharing accomplishments, and discussing project strategies.

- Knowledge specialists covering topics like design thinking or culture development, where it is beneficial to talk to an expert in the field.

Wise Words

She was once advised, "It's not only about the skill sets; understanding who you know and who trusts you are indicators for getting ahead in your career." A senior manager shared, "You need to be loyal to people, but not necessarily a company." As she built her network via the strong suggestion of a trusted colleague, she observed people with networks get the contracts and the jobs. She wished she had known this sooner.

While working on her MBA full time, Ann's intention was to move beyond her past role of chemical engineering at an agricultural commodities company. She etched a bull's-eye on brand management at the world's largest consumer goods corporation. It was notoriously difficult to get hired at this company. With an undergraduate degree in engineering and no background in marketing, she saw an opportunity to use her recent education as a launch pad to change industries and roles. The situation, however, was complicated by a shaky economy and competition with other candidates more qualified with marketing skills (on paper).

Ann tackled her interview process with her preferred choice company at the interchange of company knowledge and emotional intelligence:

- Through her networking contacts and cold calls, she contacted several current employees.

- Taking special note of employee backgrounds, she narrowed in on people with chemical engineering degrees who made the switch from engineering to product management. Understanding how they made the switch gave Ann an inside track in how to market herself to the company.

- She researched the industry and studied recent company research reports, uncovering her transferrable knowledge from one industry to another.

- Ann received valuable feedback about the company by drafting a list of smart, strategic questions composed while gathering her extensive company research.

Not surprisingly, Ann received a sales job offer from her target company by engaging in relevant and insightful conversations with current employees. With her eye on marketing, she quickly moved into brand management by cultivating relevant department relationships.

Today, Ann does not worry about a formal relationship with a long-term mentor; rather, she obtains her feedback incrementally, on demand. Her desire for feedback is situational, dependent upon circumstances. When the need arises, she contacts a specific person or any one of her diverse group of advisors.

Curated Think Tanks

Feedback agility, where real-time information is used to adapt and innovate, depicts one aspect of Ann's quest for future-proofing her career. As a meticulous researcher and design thinker in her innovation practice, she values customer feedback on new and existing products. She parlays her talent of getting to the truth behind behavior through a vigilant pursuit of real-time research.

Ann applies the same rigor of customer analysis to self-awareness and self-improvement activities.

Similar to the pop-up shop trend for promoting and testing new ideas and products by retailers, Ann launched a series of influencer salons by special invitation only. A Socratic learning method involving productive debate and well-constructed questions happens in a collaborative environment uniquely designed by Ann.

Her carefully curated salons include a mix of people who gather to deepen dialogue around specific topics like leadership, situational awareness, fashion, and shopper marketing. Her curated think tanks follow the format of:

- Topic summaries
- Identification of issues, trends, and problems
- Trend insights
- Innovative application of ideas to work and life
- Questions for the future

For those of you familiar with the design thinking process, her format is similar. They are comprised of short bursts of creative problem solving, preceded by a situation overview and problem statement.

Securing a spot at one of her influencer salons is a thrilling invitation to learn about a topic and engage in creative dialogue.

The experience benefits participants by giving them a chance to explore aspects of their personal and professional lives. At a recent salon, one person identified gaps in her career resume. She was unprepared for the serious consequences of not applying an aggressive "mobile" filter to her marketing strategy and business points of view.

Straight Talk

During a conversation with Ann, she shared some guiding principles. Ann candidly admits her unrelenting hunger for uncovering the best cultural fit between her and the companies she takes on as clients. She does not always get it right. Yet that does not stop her from learning from mistakes, making adjustments, and trying again.

According to Ann, large corporations have demonstrated the critical nature of values alignment. Many top performers were given the boot when they did not support the core values of an organization. Her discerning advice to other careerists is: spend at least 15 percent of your time on thinking and asking questions, with the goal of becoming better and doing better. She further adds, "Study and assimilate the core values of your work environment."

In addition to keeping skill sets current, Ann holds nothing back when she states, "You have to look current." As a career pro with strong brand training from one of the top consumer brands in the world, she urges workers to invest in contemporary clothing appropriate for a particular role, company, or industry. She heeds her own advice. Those St. John knits? Worn when appropriate. Casual chic guided by artsy expression, modern sporty flair, or career woman savvy by designer Maria Pinto are cycled into the lineup of personal brand expression.

Hanging out at SOHO House, a professional club with an eclectic mix of creative business members, she absorbs contemporary trends and expands her ever-evolving network. As a purveyor of an extensive number of club events ranging from meditation to self-defense to the future of work, Ann immerses herself in learning and feedback opportunities. Self-proclaimed as a work in progress, she is open to refinement ideas on the path to improvement.

She's the one in the room asking the thought-provoking questions. Take note, and start building a list of your own.

Wide Open Thinking

Obtaining feedback is easier than ever. There is a diverse assortment of options for creating feedback loops for the purpose of fine tuning and improvement. In reviewing various feedback strategies, there is one systemic trend driving equal opportunity access and sharing: open source.

Eavesdropping on conversations within coffee shops about tech culture and trends, I hear the phrase, "Yeah, that is a thing." The thing, originating in the domain of software engineering and now a mainstream concept, is open source mentality. In software circles, open source starts with source code that anyone can inspect, modify, and enhance to create software products. The code is made freely available for anyone to create new products and ideas.

Open source thinking applied in a broader context breeds innovation, fuels the sharing economy, and kindles collaboration. Sharing ideas and unsolved problems with people across borders, away from myopic silos of traditional corporations, results in inventive problem solving.

Sharing medical research at a global level, rather than hoarding the data from studies, to more quickly eradicate a disease is an effective example of smart collaboration. Another example includes organizations in tech industries (e.g., mobile) that exist to solve interoperability issues through standards, making it easier for customers. Disparate systems must work together.

The idea and feedback exchanges are a distinct advantage for global workers. People engaged at the center of sharing networks, rather than in the isolated labs of non-collaboration, will advance their careers.

Feedback Labs Among Us

Without an official sanctioned mentor established through corporate or personal connections, I discovered new ways to tap into brilliance and practical advice.

There are multiple ways you can access feedback, regardless of your lineage or station in life. The feedback loop is self-directed, giving you permission to soar among the ranks of MVPs, moving the metrics on the improvement dashboard.

Here is a collection of ideas to expand your reach for feedback:

1. Learn from dead people.

2. Crowdsource feedback on social platforms: Quora, Facebook, LinkedIn, Slack, and various platform sites.

3. Join a group: business, accountability, feedback, or special interest.

4. Embrace mentorship.

5. Establish a career advisory board with rotating or fixed members: peers, younger workers, senior leaders, or thought leaders in your industry.

6. Hire a coach: business, performance, or life.

7. Take an assessment test: self-awareness, work style, brand, or strengths.

8. Help others.

Let's explore each of these eight concepts in more detail.

FEEDBACK SQUAD

@Konstant Change

1. Learn from dead people.

Learning from enlightened people who have gone before us yet pondered similar questions is a practical way to grab a burst of inspiration. Reading books and passages or researching quote themes online enables you to savor sage advice to help solve a burdensome problem. Wisdom from famous philosophers, musicians, or family members dear to us who have passed on provides perspective.

When I asked my friend Paula Weigel about role models in her life, she immediately responded, "Mother Teresa and Gandhi." There are countless lessons and answers in the stories of their lives.

With Paula's prompting, I posed the question to myself and examined the wisdom of people no longer on this planet. The well-worn advice given to me by my Aunt Cele Gilmore, food chemist and inventor, brought a smile to my face. As the first woman in the research lab of a global company, Cele created the formulas for eight food patents, including the earliest formulation of Reddi-wip. Like the character Peggy Olson on the show *Mad Men*, whose aspirations were hampered by social norms, she endured limitations before achievement. Cele's sharp sense of corporate protocol, diligent work ethic, and personal measured responses in the face of blatant discrimination inspired my respect. When she shared stories, I listened.

During a time of employee management struggles, I urgently posed the following question to Cele: What can I do to secure more accountability from a talented member of my staff? Not certain whether my issue was one of delegation or something else, she listened carefully to the details.

She responded by simply saying, "Make her a manager." I followed Cele's advice and was rewarded with a motivated employee who took her own career to the next level.

What I learned during my time with Cele straddles professional development and leadership training. Assigning capable people more responsibility establishes trust and dances merrily down the path of accountability.

Cele's poignant reality check about job search still makes me chuckle. I could hear the emotion in my voice while sharing the eventual wonders of my life if only a particular job offer came through. Everything would be perfect, if only . . . She replied, "I don't know about this job, but my wish is you will land the 'right' job." Not exactly what I wanted to hear, but it's just what I needed.

My aunt's wise observation taught me to aim for right-fit roles, rather than obsess over first-impression dream jobs. I learned to dig deeper, interviewing the company with the same rigor they applied when interviewing me. By the way, I did not get that job, but obtained an opportunity with a strong culture and a boss who cultivated my abilities and leadership skills.

Although she is no longer alive, I "listen" to Cele's advice when faced with a crucial decision or when a reality check is in order.

There are other valuable points of view from people whose words live beyond their time on earth. I discovered three of them while doing research for this chapter:

- Failure is merely feedback that there is something blocking the path of the emergence and expansion of the best version of yourself.
  —*Mother Teresa*

- Get a feedback loop and listen to it. When people give you feedback, cherish it and use it.
  —*Randy Pausch, professor of computer science, human-computer interaction, and design; author of* Last Lecture

- If I have seen further, it is by standing on the shoulders of giants.
  —*Sir Isaac Newton*

These timeless bits of advice, wisdom, and encouragement are applicable to a wide variety of circumstances and are available 24/7.

2. Crowdsource feedback.

A valuable asset of your conversational toolkit is the nuanced knack for asking good questions. Posing smart questions will get you noticed in the workplace and lead to thoughtful insights.

Asking for advice starts with open-ended questions. Like a skillful reporter, think of who, what, where, when, how, or why questions to get to reasons behind answers or to capture context. Only use a yes/no or multiple choice approach when taking a poll, as in choosing between three design options for your personal website.

Fortunately, no-cost or low-cost online feedback options give new meaning to the phrase "Inquiring minds want to know." The crowdsource movement has inspired numerous user-generated social platforms for asking and answering questions.

The curious effect of the crowd is people genuinely want to help each other solve problems. I have witnessed an impressive generosity of input for individuals trying to make decisions for their careers or their businesses.

Consider Facebook, LinkedIn, Quora, Slack channels, and MetaFilter as a selection of places to ask questions and interact with professionals regarding career and entrepreneur topics. Many thought leaders build their communities by answering questions related to their area of expertise. You can engage with a global conglomeration of peers, entrepreneurs, coaches, and a diverse group of subject matter experts. With large online communities, you will likely receive a number of pertinent responses.

Facebook Group Example

As an entrepreneur, I often look for guidance and advice from thought leaders who publish online content, offer training, or manage Facebook groups. Chris Brogan, CEO of Owner Media Group, provides skill training for the modern entrepreneur. His community includes careerists, solopreneurs, freelancers, micro-businesses, and small businesses.

One of Chris's many productive outlets for free content sharing is a user-driven private Facebook group. With close to fifteen thousand business-focused members, questions receive several useful responses.

For example, there was a dialogue about a job seeker's interviewing process. The responders deliberated on the appropriate number of callback interviews and provided context for when the number seemed excessive.

The discussion also addressed a trend by some employers asking a job candidate to create a hypothetical program plan to demonstrate their value in the role. Group members expressed concern potential employers might be using this process for idea generation, especially if five or six candidates were delivering the same project.

Private Facebook groups are a consistent resource to gauge feedback on various subjects. I recently queried a couple Facebook groups to get feedback on the most effective messages for my new website. The value gained was significant because several members asked deeper questions about my business.

The feedback helped to clarify my position and encouraged me to make adjustments on the content. The back and forth process within groups mimics the feedback loop found with business coaching relationships.

Additional data points are a tremendous support for moving your project or career forward.

Q&A with Quora

Founded in 2009, this social platform is gaining in popularity. Quora is a question and answer site. Many of the subject matter experts I admire are active on the platform. Their one-on-one coaching may not be available as a business offering, yet you can learn from them through monitoring their answers. If you are lucky, one of them will answer your question!

The site is edited and organized by a community of users. Answers get voted up or down by the community. A quick search on Quora uncovered the following career questions:

- Should I stay or should I go?

- How would you answer this job interview question: Why shouldn't I hire you?

- What are the most desirable programming languages for getting hired?

- Is 30 too old for a career change?

- How can I find my hidden talents?

- What is the worst mistake you can make in salary negotiations?

- How do I change my career without losing everything?

If you are an entrepreneur or a solopreneur, or looking to jump onto the entrepreneur track, check out the question feed within small business advice:

- What million dollar businesses can I start now with just my laptop?

- If I want to become an entrepreneur, where do I start? (one hundred answers)

- What was the biggest mistake you made in your startup?
- Can a freelance writer get more gigs by answering questions at Quora?
- What are good marketing strategies for a small business?

Quora members may not be familiar with the multiple dimensions of your personal profile, making their feedback feel less applicable to you. However, you can monitor the pulse of a global population that has similar questions, deriving benefit from universal questions and answers. Quora is an effective outlet to research and gain general-purpose feedback from the crowd. Without word count limits, the exchanges feel and look like conversations.

3. Join a group.

Want to obtain a fresh perspective and enrich the ramblings of your own mind? Join a group of like-minded individuals who want to grow and make things happen in their careers.

For the purpose of career advancement and professional development, many groups and associations offer career development and education. These groups enable you to gather information and grow in your profession.

Groups come in varying shades of purpose and intent. For example, Meetup, the online platform for scheduling in-person gatherings, is the world's largest network of local self-forming groups. You can start or join groups according to your interests. There are a number of categories to choose from, such as entrepreneurship, personal development, leadership, public speaking, creativity, and personal branding. Any individual can start a group and attract similar people who want to share and learn.

The smaller subgroups of an industry organization, dedicated to a topic like accountability, are especially helpful for moving people and projects forward. During a recent women's technology forum I attended, the members launched a business planning and tracking program. Participants organized into self-directed four-person accountability groups. The groups meet weekly as a form of progress management and to brainstorm solutions to a member challenge.

My accountability group holds weekly status meetings to establish milestones and to measure progress. Each individual report is followed by one question, with the purpose of securing feedback on a pressing issue.

Community Conduit with Feedback Benefits

When you join a group, you may be fortunate to meet someone like Jeff Shuey.

Jeff is a group starter, group joiner, business developer, and community collaborator. He believes alliance development flourishes in service of others. His attitude furthers product ideas and uncovers partnership growth opportunities. He is a helper and a doer. Companies hire him because he solicits feedback from the community of partners and buyers, resulting in happy customers and more sales.

When I met Jeff at a conference for online business practitioners, he was wearing a Hawaiian shirt on a cold spring Chicago day. He was missing the flip-flops, but I was confident there was a pair hiding in his luggage. With a look favoring beach culture chic, reflecting the laid-back calm of his Seattle home, he owned his engineer geek status with a quirky half-smile.

Group interaction flows naturally within Jeff's community frame of mind. He founded a number of networking, industry, and partner organization chapters and groups. Some of his partner groups support one of the world's largest software companies.

Jeff is a master at listening and leveraging large influential networks. His connection strategies and willingness to engage in constructive dialogue benefits those looking to make progress in their careers or on their projects.

While interviewing him for this book, I learned the advantages of being in one of Jeff's various groups. He asked a few questions regarding my research and offered insights. He then wrote a summary of the Agile Career Development Model in a personal branding blog read by thousands of readers. Jeff's actions dramatically expanded the reach of the agility project, amplifying the promotion of my work.

With an engineering background, marketing-driven questions, and sales sensibilities, Jeff is a skillful business navigator. He listens deliberately and offers constructive feedback.

Joining a group with the intention of helping members of your business community is an effective way to tap into the serendipity of group participation. You might get lucky and meet someone like Jeff, a superconnector with feedback benefits.

Group Kismet

Joining a trustworthy group of like-minded people will help you clearly understand your value in the workplace and encourage the support of fellow careerists. Community developers and group members provide feedback to further ideas and expand the mission of the team.

When chatting with Andy Crestodina, a resourceful content marketer who has cornered the way to optimize online presence, he offered a clever concept. He suggested the formation of two types of groups: private Slack channel groups and participation in multiple self-directed mastermind groups.

These "safe" environments enable support and a best-practices approach to growth. The Slack team can be comprised of hundreds of members rallying around your topic, or a smaller private group. Formal commercial mastermind groups can cost thousands of dollars to participate, but Andy urges people to create their own groups and to join more than one. They can be accomplished over video chat, phone, or in person.

Collaboration creates abundance.

4. Embrace mentorship.

The formal definition of a mentor is: an experienced and trusted advisor. A mentor advises or trains (someone, especially a younger colleague).

> A mentor is someone who allows you
> to see the hope inside yourself.
> —*Oprah Winfrey*

There are two basic types:

- Workplace mentors—older and wiser advocates who guide you and have your back. Remember, this type of mentor can be elusive for many, yet they do exist in the workplace.

- Mentors in the formative years who teach you about vital skills (life, work, survival, values, ideas about success, etc.).

Workplace Mentors Nurture Possibility

Gregory Wade, a senior IT executive and software entrepreneur originally from the United States and now based in Vancouver, Canada, tells the story of his early career. He worked in operations at the world's most recognized telecommunications brand.

As Greg describes it, "My mentor saw something in me suited to customer service and sales." His mentor, a director of sales, had built a multifaceted career in this area and observed Greg's potential for growth in the areas of strategy and partner development.

Heeding advice from his mentor and leveraging off-the-charts emotional intelligence (emotional quotient/EQ), Greg learned how to develop and grow multimillion-dollar revenue partnerships. He honed his relationship development craft in the big leagues with companies like Home Depot, FedEx, and Coca-Cola. His grooming program in strategy and partnerships served as a launching pad for fast-paced career movement.

He managed a $30 million business in a director role at a mobile device and software company, advancing to senior vice president where he built a $3 billion business in Asia Pacific overseeing four hundred employees. Wow! Accomplishments like these are extraordinary. His mentor's initial assessment and encouragement opened the doors of possibility. Leaders are nurtured by the beliefs and guidance of mentors. Greg's desire to own the reins, by building and growing high-performance teams, accomplished the rest.

He attributes his career path to his mentor and believes in paying it forward by taking on mentorship roles at major Silicon Valley companies, business school groups, and individuals.

Pay It Forward

Mentorship benefits young people. Greg's volunteer coaching and mentoring with grade school and college students deepen his commitment to helping people define their value. In the spirit of questions eliciting thoughtful responses, he asks, "What is your background?" "What drives you?" "What motivates you?" and "How did your parents' views affect you?"

His agenda for these conversations is to listen and learn before giving the students a perspective of the real world. His extensive work experience on the global stage enables him to nudge students beyond their limited vantage point. He advocates the aligned path vs. the easy path.

When he met with a young man studying computer science at a Canadian university, he observed the student was fixated on becoming a programmer. This was understandable, as the student was from Mainland China, where technical skills and STEM programs are highly regarded.

Greg elaborated on the value of multilingual and listening skills, multiplying the college senior's employment choices across functions of the modern business organization. There is a growing need for East-West translation of culture and language concepts. The technology-adept student with unique language skills could also translate abstract concepts into expressions more easily understood by non-engineers.

As Greg pointed out, these skills are differentiators. He invites careerists to "be proud and take advantage of slight differences."

The keen advice he provides to all professionals includes the following:

- Follow a path where you own your destiny.
- Always have a fallback skill.

- Protect your interests by building and nurturing your network.

Music Teacher Muse

Michelle Mazur, an accomplished speaking coach with a PhD in communications, considers herself a communication rebel. She is a catalyst for entrepreneurs, business leaders, and authors to increase their effectiveness in the areas of influence, content creation, and speech delivery.

The long and winding road of roles included academic, research director, project manager, and speech coach for movers and shakers. The career expedition started in the humble halls of high school, where she met her first mentor. Preceded by a reverent pause, Michelle blurted out her high school music teacher's name: Peter Mueller.

No matter how much time has passed, most people can proudly recite the name of their first mentor quickly, first and last name.

She remembered, "He wanted us to excel." Through his teaching and behavior examples, Michelle aspired to "be all that I can be; do my best." She remarked, "He helped me do more."

Mentors and teachers matter to the impressionable minds of youth.

Never Too Early

Workplace habits start early. Charlie Gilkey, a business doer, strategist, and productivity advisor, runs a company called Productive Flourishing in Portland, Oregon. His analytical thinking and honest feedback have created a success track record for many of his clients.

Charlie's quick memory of significant mentor names included two teachers, Mr. Hendrick and Mr. Abernathy, men who served in the military. Guess what? Charlie spent ten years in the military, an incredible foundation for his approach to discipline in business.

Charlie grew up in the second poorest part of town, where violence, drugs, abuse, and broken families often resulted in dead-end lives. The mentor duo of teachers issued harsh measures of discipline, yet cultivated a safe, structured place with boundaries. Mr. Hendrick challenged them with, "No one is inherently smarter than you. You will be successful based on how successful you are in school." He was also the first black man in Charlie's life who had a master's degree. He was biracial, just like Charlie.

There was tough love, but also rewards.

The underlying message was: Work harder to get what you want, because no one was going to give you anything. As Charlie recalls, "We had to be better than everyone else. Smarter, more disciplined, and tougher."

Charlie's classes were diverse, including black, white, Vietnamese, Laotian, and Latino kids. He remarked, "The commonality of our poverty and outlooks bound us more tightly than race divided us." The poetic statement about a band of kids groomed for more than their surroundings leaves a profound impression regarding the value of mentorship.

Listening to Charlie illustrated the stunning importance of mentors, but also the willingness to listen and apply the feedback to our lives.

It's not surprising Charlie's military training and early influences led to a career covering situation analysis and business guidance. He fosters diversity of thought and has cultivated diversity in his client and student rosters. Some of his clients admit the difficulties of looking inside and paying attention to the advice. But those who do, truly flourish.

Learning from the tough guys has its rewards.

As you consider entering into a mentor/mentee relationship, you may want to adopt Charlie's commitment to paying attention and acting on the advice provided. Take a few moments to scour your memories in search of guidance from your formative years. As Charlie discovered, some of his most positive character traits were rooted long ago.

We all have opportunities to be a mentor to the impressionable minds of children. Being a mentor is a great way to learn about becoming a mentee later on in your career. The alternating positions of mentee and mentor stimulate self-awareness, creating a balance between the healthy humility of the learner and confidence of the teacher.

5. Establish a career advisory board.

The DIY movement applies to the self-directed mentor magnet. You are capable of attracting and assembling your own team. Like the pit crew at Indy, they will be there for you.

The personal advisory board, however, requires a discerning eye for talent. Just as corporations hire the best available person for the role, you will surround yourself with the best available minds to help you on your work path.

Like an agile project, your advisors will cycle through your career journey as defined by your needs. The rules of simple arithmetic apply; addition and subtraction of team members will fortify the career growth equation.

Earlier in the chapter, I described the feedback team: Feedback teams are comprised of specific mentors, or a series of people who care about your development. Your brain trust of advisors are similar to a treasured collection of souvenirs, evoking memories of your experiences, yet fostering future dreams.

Posing the question, "How can I be better?" launches a feedback squad worthy of your cultivation.

Situational Advisor

When I spoke to Hope Bertram, a content curator and conference producer of digital media summits, she described her mentorship relationships as situational. She designed and launched a summit for a new healthcare vertical, an industry deviating from her consumer product focus. Collaborating with her advisor in healthcare, Hope created a relevant slate of presenters and content for this new conference.

The launch exceeded her business forecast. She acknowledges the value of being mentored on a particular topic and does not hesitate to ask for feedback. Hope's humility about what she doesn't know, and her sincere request for guidance, attract professionals and peers who are happy to help.

Reverse Mentor/Advisor

When building out my staff at a mobile security company in 2007, I hired a young woman, Brenna Walters Lenoir, who excelled at blogging and writing. She had no formal marketing experience, as much of her time was spent in pre-med coursework. Yet I knew her blogging and uncanny relationship-building skills would serve the department well.

Over the next two years, she built the foundation for our community blogging strategy and taught me many aspects of website management. We collaborated on three corporate websites in eighteen months! There was an assumed exchange in our relationship. I taught her about marketing strategy, public relations, tradeshows, and project management. She nudged me to roll up my sleeves to explore the back end of the digital marketing world.

The reverse mentoring relationship went smoothly as I developed my skills as a marketing technologist, the next phase of career development required for the digital marketing profession.

Peer Advisor

Watching the Amazon original story called *When Good Girls Revolt*, based on real-life events, I am reminded of the importance of peer guidance. The story takes place in the 1960s at *News of the Week*, when women played subordinate roles in the newsroom of print publications. The story parallels actual events that took place at the real *Newsweek*.

Men held the reporter and editor positions, owning high-profile bylines. Women held lower level roles like researchers, fact checkers, and mail clerks. Their work was hidden from public awareness. Their command of the topic was sufficient for composing stories, yet their individuality and creativity were suppressed. Regardless of their innovative approaches and contributed writing, they were denied access to the glory of the byline.

A team of women helped each other through the wasteland of unrequited recognition as storytellers. One woman threw down the gauntlet to a colleague (in the ladies room), challenging her to write the story and claim a byline. This act posed the risk of getting fired. The character wrote the story and, when chastised, left her position in pursuit of a legitimate and visible writing job. The character was Nora Ephron. As a mail girl with high aspirations, Nora eventually crafted a distinguished career in journalism and script writing after she left *Newsweek*.

The women of *Newsweek* filed a landmark lawsuit in the early 1970s. They sued for equal access to journalism jobs, rather than being relegated to mail clerk positions and fact checker roles. Their accomplished education, viable talent, and deep desire to write were on par with their male counterparts.

A great example of peer advisors in action.

Colleagues are great confidants and can provide a welcome point of view on a challenging issue. A peer can kick us in the butt when we need to call upon a bravado spirit to achieve our goals or advance to a new role. A peer is the listener when we simply need to express our deepest fears or sadness. Expression, even frustration, can unleash the inner power of our career crusade.

6. Hire a coach.

Many successful careerists hire coaches to help them accomplish goals. Remember Greg Wade, the senior-level executive responsible for building a $3 billion business? He worked with an executive coach to build leadership skills, creating a plan to leverage strengths and mitigate his weaknesses.

According to a study by Anders Ericsson, a psychologist and scientific researcher, optimal performance on cognitive, perceptual, and motor tasks requires deliberate practice and timely feedback. In the study, he learned the quality and quantity of practice are equally important.

The premise of his work was how to become a leading expert within a particular subject area like science or at a skill like playing the violin. His findings apply to many aspects of improvement. Combining repetition of a skill by a motivated participant with immediate feedback leads to increased learning and improvement.

While skills will improve with repetition only, performance benefits from observation and insights of a coach. The time it takes to learn is compressed with feedback. Examples are one-on-one tutors to improve student progress and coaches who work with athletes to optimize their performance.

Although he does not market himself as a coach, Charlie Gilkey, mentioned earlier, advises small businesses and entrepreneurs. His clients make significant improvements in their strategies and leadership accomplishments while working with him.

There are different types of coaches; entrepreneurial, career, executive, and life are four types to consider. Many respected and visible leaders hire coaches to work on issues such as self-awareness, delegation, communication effectiveness, and leadership skills.

7. Take an assessment.

Feedback regarding your strengths and inclinations is available through use of quick and efficient online assessment tools. These survey instruments are backed by some of the top minds in psychology and human performance.

The instruction "play to your strengths" is uttered by teachers, managers, and coaches when referring to environments like the soccer field or the workplace. Yet without a coach or a formal appraisal of your true capacity, your strengths may be languishing in a hidden corner, waiting to be discovered by a random talent agent. Rather than leave this vital personal knowledge quest to a chance encounter, taking an assessment will yield useful information about you.

The truth about who we are lies somewhere between high-priced, consultant-facilitated surveys and today's equal access to digital assessment tools. Knowing your innate abilities and instincts is a self-awareness directive for the confident career challenger. The resulting profile often provides a surprisingly accurate reflection of you in the areas of style, personality, strengths, weaknesses, and attitudes, to name a few.

While there are a variety of low-cost or no-cost tools, let's take a look at a few assessment tool options:

Myers-Briggs Type Indicator

Derived from Carl Jung's work on psychological types, this one has been around since the 1920s and is a type of personality test. The first questionnaire was published in 1943, co-developed by Katharine Cook Briggs and her daughter Isabel Briggs Myers. Classifications like ENTJ or INFP let people know where they fall on the scale of introversion/extroversion, sensing/intuition, thinking/feeling, and judging/perceiving. There are sixteen archetypes.

Kolbe Index

Created by Kathy Kolbe, a leading authority on human instincts, this index is based on instincts, rather than personality and intelligence. The results help people understand their own instinctive strengths. When working in a group, it is useful to understand the strengths of all team members. Kolbe testing helps you understand the talent you were born with and how to be your best self. Designations include fact-finder, follow-through, quick start, and implementer.

Keirsey Temperament Sorter

Inspired by the ancient study of temperament by Hippocrates and Plato, this seventy-question survey, originally launched in 1956 by David Keirsey, is a personality test. People are organized based on temperaments: artisan, guardian, idealist, and rational. The sixteen different personality types correlate to the personality types of Myers-Briggs.

StrengthsFinder

This one has been quite popular since the book was published in 2007. Gallup studied and created the science of strengths. Strategy and career development workshops across the country encourage participants to take the test to understand what they are best at. By answering a few questions on the Clifton StrengthsFinder, people can make choices about their life's work, playing to their strengths. This tool does not focus on weaknesses.

Fascination Advantage Assessment

Created by Sally Hogshead in 2010, the Fascination Advantage is a personality-profiling tool that shows you how the world sees you, rather than how you see the world. As an advertising executive turned career optimizer, she teamed up with researchers to develop the system. The profile platform takes a cue from brand development protocol, where a brand is defined by the experience of the customer. There are a total of forty-nine possible archetypes. The tool is used for individuals and small businesses.

Assessment Abundance

The path to self-awareness reminds me of Hermann Hesse's 1922 novel *Siddhartha*, about a man's journey to self-discovery during the time of the Gautama Buddha. While Siddhartha's long and complicated journey required much sacrifice to uncover his own truth, we can take smaller steps to understand our values and strengths.

While profile summaries are not a shortcut to being the best possible you, they will provide context for playing to your strengths as you contemplate a decision. From a marketing perspective, many of the phrases and words reflected in the profiles can serve as content or copy inspiration as you position your unique contribution in the workplace.

With the heightened focus of personal branding and the ongoing hunt for right-fit careers, there are countless online measurement tools. Use the word "assessment" in your search query to yield a variety of personal assessment options. If you have not tried one, give it a test drive. You may uncover a superpower in your portfolio of talents.

8. Help others.

Look beyond your immediate surroundings and personal agendas. You will notice a more balanced view of the world and start to gain a better understanding of you. Rewards are multiplied when you collaborate with or help others.

When a manager develops his staff, the department experiences benefits like increased productivity and individual well-being. Here are the perspectives of a few thought leaders on the concept:

- Steve Farber, the author of *The Radical Leap: A Personal Lesson in Extreme Leadership*, opens many of his speeches and training with, "Do what you love in service of people who love what you do."

- Legions of individuals believe in the servant leadership concept, first cultivated by Robert Greenleaf. The leadership belief is: a philosophy and set of practices that enriches the lives of individuals, builds better organizations and ultimately creates a more just and caring world.

- As Greg Wade, the technology exec mentor, so eloquently communicated, "Giving back is the cornerstone of developing others and creating an optimal work culture and increasing potential."

We are surrounded by leadership stories in support of a better workplace. As we teach others to strike the self-awareness chord, we gain a better understanding of ourselves in the process. We devour wisdom gained while helping people. Self-knowledge enhances leadership.

How many times have you heard people express, "I learned more in the process of teaching than I did as a student?" or "I gained more in the process of giving."

When I was at a low point, deep in the recesses of self-doubt and negative self-talk in my personal life, something magnificent happened. In the middle of a devastating divorce, when self-esteem was difficult to muster, a friend offered the suggestion, "Help someone."

Taking this to heart, I cofounded a divorce support group with others struggling to turn their lives around. The real secret to my best self was reflected back weekly via the remarkable insights of generous new friends.

Helping people creates a feedback mirror where you can view an authentic reflection of you. Insights gained through generous efforts make a lasting imprint in your mind.

Summary
Yikes! That's a whole lotta feedback goin' on!

Eight different types of feedback may overwhelm your calendar and time-management sensibilities. Yet one or two of these methods may be an appropriate fit for your personal style.

With an eye on creativity, growth, and happiness, conscious feedback seekers excel in the sphere of human performance.

As the Swedish psychologist Anders Ericsson said, deliberate practice demands feedback to maximize expert performance. The act of focused repetition of a task or a skill, accentuated by constructive critique, will accelerate mastery.

The productive road to betterment and beyond is in your grasp. As Ken Blanchard, a management expert and prolific author, shares, "Feedback is the breakfast of champions." I'd say it's time to be selective with your breakfast menu.

Next Steps

Let's review the eight suggestions for obtaining feedback along the career path.

Feedback methods:

1. Learn from dead people.
2. Crowdsource feedback on social platforms: Quora, Facebook, LinkedIn, Slack Channels, and various crowdsource platform sites.
3. Participate in one or more groups: business, accountability, feedback, or specialty.
4. Embrace mentorship.
5. Establish a career advisory board with rotating or fixed members: peers, younger workers, senior leaders, or thought leaders in your industry.
6. Hire a coach: business, performance, or life.
7. Take an assessment test: self-awareness, work style, brand, or strengths.
8. Help others.

Exercises

1. Complete the following sentence: If I could change one thing about my current work situation, I

would _____. Pick two of the feedback methods to help you solve this workplace issue or career challenge. Get comfortable asking for help. Keep track of your observations and results for ninety days. Create a summary of your findings and share with a trusted friend/advisor.

2. Create a wise words sheet by analyzing advice from people from the past. Apply the words to your current situation.

3. Help one person (mentee, colleague, or friend) by listening to his career challenges. Put yourself in his shoes, as he defines the problem. Make sure you understand the problem before responding. Provide thoughts and observations in the form of feedback. Consider this an opportunity to become part of a fellow careerist's feedback squad.

CHAPTER 8

Principle Seven: Think of Your Career as a Series of Projects

Somehow, I always thought of my career as a series of projects, not jobs.
— *SETH GODIN, AUTHOR, ENTREPRENEUR,*
MARKETER, AND PROFESSIONAL SPEAKER

The Career Ecosystem of Tectonic Shifts

When tectonic plates shift beneath the earth's surface, there are frequently a series of geological events like volcanic eruptions, earthquakes, avalanches, and tsunamis. After a period of adjustment, analysis, and response, communities rebuild and adapt to the revised landscape.

The ecosystem of employers, employees, and free agents rumbles across the surface of inevitable change. Just like the aftereffects of an earthquake, companies and individuals must accommodate the impact of globalization, technology trends, and economic shifts. Starting with a scramble to stabilize their footing, they gradually calibrate their position in the realigned environment.

The Alliance Between Employer and Employee

In the employer universe, when adverse effects hit the bottom line, the variable most subject to change is staffing levels. Companies are becoming more lean and agile. With a downsizing trigger in effect on the corporate side, many workers are adapting to the new rules and taking responsibility for their own path.

According to an article titled "Tours of Duty" by Reid Hoffman, Ben Casnocha, and Chris Yeh, the alliance between employer and employees is healthy if both sides seek to add value to the other. The authors state, "Employees invest in the company's adaptability, while the company invests in the employees' employability."

This new alliance assumes professional development and training for employees who are no longer seen as threats as they build their personal brands and value in the broader marketplace. In complementary fashion, capable, competent, and well-trained employees add value to the employer.

This type of career agility enables individuals to be more marketable with greater access to opportunities within their current company or in the external business environment.

Revisiting the definition of career agility, agile careerists optimize their life's work on three levels: creativity, growth, and happiness. Employers must deliver this value to maintain balance in the new alliance.

As businesses adapt to change, the employer plays the flexibility card by hiring or firing talent as needed to accommodate the workload. The traditional model of employment, where the employer had the upper hand in the relationship, has shifted to a more equitable state.

The career consequences of the shift have inspired individual growth spurts, generated new learning opportunities, and triggered shorter lengths of stay at each role.

Millennials Not Alone in Reduced Job Tenure

The most noteworthy trend resulting from the altered state of the new alliance is reduced job tenure.

Like a flashing warning light at an intersection admonishing the driver to take notice, job tenure is declining across corporations. A few years back, many articles were written about the short attention span of millennials in the workplace. According to the US Bureau of Labor Statistics in 2016, however, boomers and Gen Xers have joined them in the march to shorter lengths of stay across corporate campuses.

Growth Spurts and Job Tenure

Ric Dragon, with soulful brown eyes and sporting an Irish tweed cap, embodies the notion of staying as long as necessary. As I will illustrate through Ric's story, the length of stay is self-directed, determined by learning opportunities and interest. Ric has lived the roles of information architect, web search consultant, author, speaker, business strategist, musician, web application developer, marketer, online marketing firm business owner, and artist.

Although Ric's central identity is artist, following are a couple examples highlighting his sequence of learning, personal evolution, and job roles:

Web Application Developer

Ric refers to compressed learning experiences accompanied by deep focus as high-density learning. In this accelerated approach to accumulating knowledge, he learned how to apply his talent in art and design to web applications and web development.

His timing was perfect. He was part of a growing group of innovators who mastered web development when access to computing resources was being democratized. He helped bring businesses online via the internet.

Work and career projects flowing out of his high-density experiences spurred energy and momentum as he adapted to the new rules of each newfound profession.

Digital Strategy for Business Growth

While designing web applications, he met an organizational development professional who introduced him to business ideas, a series of fundamental business books, and publications like McKinsey & Company reports and *Harvard Business Review*. With the same fervor displayed in previous pursuits, he absorbed the concepts of competitive forces and how companies transition from good to great.

Ric built a strong foundation of business skills that would rival most MBA thinkers, enabling him to build a leading digital strategy company. Each of his compressed learning experiences cycled into jobs and roles where he expanded his portfolio of skills.

His lifelong interest in learning and creating art on the side evolved to the next phase of his career: exploring (and making) abstract art and music in Bogota, Columbia.

Which brings us to our next principle of viewing your career as a series of projects.

Principle Seven: Think of Your Career as a Series of Projects

The dictionary definition of a project is: an individual or collaborative enterprise that is carefully planned and designed to achieve a particular aim. Additionally, it is "a specific task of investigation." A project suggests deadlines and marshals your resources toward accomplishment.

The marathon runner often thinks of his race as a series of shorter races, rather than the daunting task of twenty-six miles.

Let's discuss the principle.

Your Career as a Series of Projects Principle

Think of job roles as two- to three-year projects building on your incremental knowledge. Harness the enthusiasm of a fresh start, master the job, and build new competencies. Become the most eligible employee for promotion or the best candidate at another company, or launch your personal startup project.

Shorter tenure and a project mentality flavor your work with urgency and purpose. This experience can be observed in the new venture process at startup accelerators, where the average length from startup idea definition to building the product is three months. These accelerated efforts and compressed timeframes stimulate innovation.

Who wouldn't want to get started on and/or finish a project?

Conquering Chaos

When I was director of marketing at a network management software company, the disorganized chaos of our growth-stage company threatened further progress. At fifty employees, the leadership team attempted to tame our departmental independent streaks. The early-stage habits of decision making through gut instincts and working long days to compensate for missed deadlines risked startup burnout.

CAREER AS A SERIES OF PROJECTS

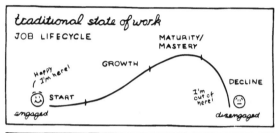

traditional state of work
JOB LIFECYCLE

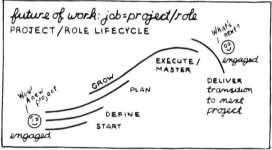

future of work: job=project/role
PROJECT/ROLE LIFECYCLE

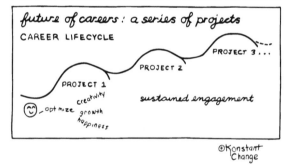

future of careers: a series of projects
CAREER LIFECYCLE

©Konstant
Change

The new vice president of engineering, having recently worked at a Fortune 500 company, recognized the lack of formal processes across the company. He implemented a training workshop for managers, covering formal project management skills and processes.

The instructor grabbed our attention with the captivating story about how the decision to put a man on the moon was made possible through project management. When President

John F. Kennedy's moon shot speech on May 25, 1961, promised to put an American on the moon by the end of the decade, NASA's program leaders responded.

With no shortage of anxiety in their collective gasp, leaders rallied their teams with a structured approach to achieving ambitious goals.

The team generated high-level phases and a series of milestones, organizing a considerable group of program and project managers. These individuals collaborated with engineers, scientists, management, and clerical workers to move the long-term project forward.

During the course, we learned a massive, gutsy presidential goal could be accomplished only by breaking it down into milestone phases. Here is an example:

- Phase one: Create spacecraft for testing flight
- Phase two: Fly to the moon
- Phase three: Orbit the moon with unmanned spacecraft
- Phase four: Learn about the moon's environment and establish safety requirements for humans via satellite program
- Phase five: Test Apollo equipment, orbiting the moon with manned spacecraft
- Phase six: Land an unmanned spacecraft on the moon
- Phase seven: Land a manned spacecraft on the moon and fly safely back to earth

The long-term project was further separated into multiple operations. To ensure success and safety, the managers coordinated these areas: program control, system engineering, testing, reliability and quality, and flight operations.

Some of these phases and accompanying milestones required sequential efforts, while other phases were handled concurrently.

The goal was accomplished on July 20, 1969, via the Apollo 11 voyage, within the timeframe established by President Kennedy.

Celestial Inspiration

This historical celestial example of project management forever altered my fear of organizing and accomplishing large-scale workplace tasks. The breakdown of complicated programs into smaller sections tempered the perpetual full-plate syndrome, calming the panic induced by endless piles of work.

With my brain no longer scattered in my endless workflow, I relished the rhythm of new beginnings and completions. This pattern created a cycle of satisfaction and engagement with my work.

Rather than coming to work every day to finish one more task on a very long list, individuals who embrace project management skills will control their workload. The villain of focus is distraction. By focusing on bite-size pieces of the project, workers stay productive.

During my tenure at tech companies, I taught the basics of project management to new marketers. For new employees, there was often a gap between the idea stages and planning of their work to execution of projects. With a new-worker bias toward the idea stages, the predictable missing pieces of the equation included spreadsheets, process structure, time estimates, and project tracking. Without this structure, deadlines were slippery.

The first reaction by employees more familiar with organic creative development was resistance to the deliberate constraints of organization. Eventually, the practical frameworks wrangled their way into the minds of the unsuspecting converts. As marketers dove into their newly acquired profession, there was a distinct sigh of relief as they exerted a sense of control over their workload and personal time.

Like stories with a beginning, middle, and end, projects are alive with the promise of launching something new and bringing it to completion. Similar to every story, there is a hero who experiences the arc of the project journey, brimming with work, inevitable setbacks, and the nimble pulse of a creative problem solver.

Develop Your Story Hero: Apply a Project Filter to Your Career

Since project management methods boost productivity, increase focus, and show progress, why not apply the practice to individual career management?

Sample project steps for career management include:

- Break down long and sometimes daunting career paths into manageable segments of time.

- Complete and reflect on significant milestones demonstrating accomplishment through personal and professional growth.

- Assemble a portfolio of job capabilities and competencies.

- Make incremental adjustments to career based on key learnings from each project.

According to project managers, elevated focus and progress tracking are the side benefits of productivity. A project mentality stimulates individual focus while reinforcing the ability to control activities required for moving milestones and tasks forward.

The first step to applying a project filter to your work journey starts by organizing the uninterrupted long-haul view of your life's work into manageable segments.

Rather than staring into the abyss, you can "Keep Calm and Carry On" with a tidy picture of next steps. The popular culture hijacking of this motivational phrase from British WWII posters summarizes yet another benefit of project management.

Better to be calm than harried!

Forging the Future

The quote for this chapter starts with:

> Somehow, I always thought of my career as a series of projects, not jobs.
> —Seth Godin

What comes to mind when you hear the word "project"?

When hearing this word in the workplace, I imagine science project, research project, special projects, or task force, among others. Coupled with leadership mandates, these phrases combine to elevate the importance of the activity.

With this idea, Seth Godin, an author, entrepreneur, marketer, and professional speaker, was at the forefront of launching personal projects as a career plan. When combined, this series of projects form an impressive collection of twenty books, business ventures, employee experiences, and online learning platforms.

As a portfolio careerist who lines up an assortment of jobs to fortify incremental capabilities, Seth increases the value of his lifetime accomplishments with each new project. His latest venture is an altMBA program, an intense, online four-week learning workshop focused on enabling leaders to advance in their careers. Students of his program include an impressive array of senior leadership from across the globe.

Known for innovative marketing concepts like Permission Marketing and the Ideavirus, online content that spreads rapidly, Seth Godin hatches ideas at hyperspeed. His community development concept of building tribes of devoted followers to grow online businesses has established Seth as an inspirational marketing futurist.

Lessons from the Project Champion

Seth Godin penned a blog post titled "Thirty Years of Projects," a list of every initiative since he held his first job. While he makes the distinction between personal projects vs. projects for others (employers), his enthusiasm for each new venture is evident.

He makes a strong argument for impassioned independent worker and freelancer paths. Yet his project approach easily translates to the life of an agile careerist, whether an individual works for an employer, launches a business, or becomes a contract consultant.

Let's take a look at some of the characteristics, behaviors, and attitudes stimulated by working on a project:

- Shorter time span
- Higher engagement

- Ownership initiative
- Sustained momentum vs. inevitable protracted slumps from the long haul
- Increased focus
- Heightened productivity
- Reduced boredom
- Projects as learning opportunities

Some of these benefits are dependent on the type of project, yet I think many of us can relate to the day we started a new job or shifted to a special role.

Do you remember the feeling of excitement? Your email inbox was probably close to zero, establishing your fresh slate status, clearing the way for positive expectations. Launching something new and meeting different faces in your workplace sparked creative ideas as you shaped work plans.

Projected Culture Shift

New jobs bring steep learning curves. The unexpected energy and efforts experienced in this productive state of mind are ideal for the employee AND employer.

Considering the crisis of fading employee engagement at work, the workplace could benefit from a project framework. The yearly Gallup poll continues to report less than 33 percent of workers are engaged.

As Seth Godin pointed out in his post, the "workplace culture is shifting from one of long-term affiliations (jobs) to projects." The analysts confirm his assessment, as a Freelancers Union survey from 2016 reports 35 percent of the US workforce, fifty-five million, are doing freelance work. This number is expected to escalate to 40 percent by 2020, sixty million people, according to a study by Intuit. These workers are focused on project work as their full-time occupation or as side gigs.

Seth's reference to the independent worker and the freelance economy complements the 2016 Bureau of Labor Statistics report. Specifically, these two data points highlight the similarities between shorter tenure across all generations and a project mentality.

A project mindset is resident in the domains of free agents and employees who work at companies.

Let's dig deeper into a model of corporate career management consistent with framing jobs as projects. Uncovering this next body of work solved the puzzle of my historical career choices, anchoring my commitment to agility in the workplace.

Tours of Duty as Projects

A project view exists in the minds of freelancers and corporate employees alike. Projects mark the milestones of achievement benefitting individuals interested in employability and organizations seeking growth.

In 2013 the *Harvard Business Review* "Tours of Duty" article, authored by the triangle team of Reid Hoffman, Founder of LinkedIn, Ben Casnocha, and Chris Yeh, was published. The following year, the concepts were further explored in their book, *The Alliance: Managing Talent in the Networked Age*.

When Reid Hoffman first started LinkedIn, he established two- to four-year tours of duty for new employees. This is the length of time it takes for a product development cycle or for a worker to complete a program. These incremental alliances between employer and employee establish realistic commitments, spurring enthusiastic and dedicated engagement over shorter tenure.

As the idea matured, alternate tours of duty emerged. The tours included: rotational for entry-level workers (one to three years), transformational for employees focused on a specific mission (two to four years), and foundational (variable) for mission-critical employees.

Tours are potentially renewable, with individuals taking on a different role or advancing a program within the company. With a "my work is done here" sentiment, some workers will move to another company, using the length of stay to expand knowledge and fortify skills. In the case of a departure decision, and assuming the tour of duty was a good fit for the worker, marketability increased during the tour of duty.

Inherent in the alliance, and true to the roots of LinkedIn as the business world's first successful social network, is creation and nurturing of employee and external networks. Creation of transferrable skills and confirming value of the individual to an industry or broader market are vital variables of the alliance.

How do people create projects or tours of duty at companies and string them together for the best possible career story? Let's find out by learning from a woman whose flexible perspective and resilient attitude achieved impressive career milestones.

Right Brain Left Brain @ Work

Although this concept is a bit of a neurological myth, most people identify with the characteristics of right-brain or left-brain thinking. There are a number of individuals who fall in the middle of the spectrum. Like analogies bookended by extremes, humans fall somewhere on a scale between these category titles.

A right-brain thinker is said to be creative, curious, and intuitive. A left-brain thinker tends to be more logical, strategic, and rational.

Karen Stephenson integrates both characteristics into her personality.

As a boomer business owner, she covers three topics in her Facebook feed and never breaks the forbidden barriers of religion or politics. Her consistent daily content is at the top of my preference list. She shares:

- Home style and women's fashion clothing and apparel—pictures and commentary
- Business articles about her industry
- Photos from daily runs and walks

Creative Flair

She anchors her classic look with dark-framed glasses and shoulder-length black hair. She often tames her full mane by wearing a low ponytail or a French twist and has been known to literally wear many hats: fur (Russian), baseball, beret, fedora, and wide-brim, among others.

She looks like she could be a close relative of Kate Middleton, Duchess of Cambridge. Her style is elegant and tailored, with a flair for shoes and boots.

Business Focus

Her trim physique and slight stature contrast her mighty business persona. As CEO of a burgeoning senior care services franchise, she reflects a strong yet empathetic leader in a caring business requiring tact and business management finesse.

Other posts in her stream include advocacy for senior citizens via personal television interviews. Her recent live video covered how to calm anxious family members afflicted with Alzheimer's. She shares relevant industry articles, contributing insights and comments to the posts.

Now that you have a sense of Karen's style and business background, how did a project mentality benefit her career choices? I've divided her career into phases and iterative competencies to illustrate the principle of careers as a series of projects.

Career Phases as Projects

1. Childhood Learning, Stock Sales, Insurance

Karen's curiosity about the sales process started early.

She learned the ups and downs of sales and the stock market via her father's line of work selling stocks and insurance. As a nine-year-old, she visited his office after school and helped to write out the orders for the stock transactions. Her father's inquisitive apprentice once rode in the car with him and attended a few sales calls.

The discipline of steady effort and the long view of building a business impressed her. Her parents instilled a hard work attitude by establishing a regimen of indoor and outdoor weekly chores.

Her mother nourished Karen's creative side by teaching her about decorating, design, and fashion. Karen's mother enlisted her in creative projects at an early age. Her mother was a competent seamstress, sewing all the clothes for herself and her three daughters. She taught Karen how to design her own patterns and also to sew them. She collaborated with her daughters on art and interior design in their home.

Skills: financial numbers, sales, adapt to volatility, design, work ethic

2. Social Worker for Families in Crisis

With a degree in social work, Karen worked as a social worker where she advanced her listening skills. She mastered the dual arts of in-depth listening and intuition in an environment requiring probing questions and persistent digging. She learned to look beyond the obvious answers to help people in need.

Skills: active listening, desire to help, empathy, intuition, asking the right questions with a probing style

3. Talent Recruiter for Corporate Roles

The social work environment required too long a cycle for bottom-line impact to satisfy Karen's work style. She desired to see the results of her work on a shorter timeline. Her desire for movement and activity guided her to the next phase in her career path. With her extra inner drive in full throttle, she landed in the talent recruiting business.

Karen refined her listening and conversation skills to earn a top spot on a national sales force of a recruiting agency. This role was a combination of matchmaking and helping others. She used her foundation skills to pose the right questions, customizing them based on the behavior of the candidate. This turned out to be a winning approach.

She routinely shattered the sales numbers and planted her feet firmly in the sales profession.

Skills: tenacity, empathy, making cold calls, refined active listening skills, reflecting behavior of candidates by posing insightful questions, sales process fundamentals

4. Technology and Software Sales

Karen did not see a lot of growth for the long haul in recruiting executive assistants for talent agencies. With an agile mindset, she craved professional growth and aspired to be in a high-growth, high-energy line of business. Big league sales!

Using her broader knowledge about the vertical markets in the recruiting field, she observed the impending landslide of the computer and software industries. She desired to be in an industry with an upward arc in the next phase of her life's work. Karen applied her escalating sales talents to the marketing and sales of technology and software for fast-growing companies.

Karen held multiple roles for various technology firms, ranging from account development to sales executive with regional and national territories. She became expert at opening new business opportunities, moving from business developer to sales closer.

She managed the tough competition and earned high rewards in software systems sales, generating notable wealth and savings for her growing family.

Skills: competitive analysis, earning customer trust, long-term relationship development, technical knowledge interpretation, business systems knowledge, customer requirements development, sales closing

5. General Construction, Project Management, Consumer Renovation Industry

Using her personal home renovation management as a prototype project and flexibility for raising children as a driver, Karen started a general construction company. The travel requirements and intensity of senior sales positions resulted in burnout for a divorced mother of two. Karen was ready for a new project!

Reviewing the principle of a career as a series of projects, Karen's audit of her transferable skills included sales and marketing planning. Her early design skills, augmented by empathy, a helping manner from her social work experience, and listening abilities, converged as her distinct advantage in the next role. The portfolio of iterative career skills formed an ideal platform for managing customer rehab construction projects.

While not as financially successful as the sales part of her career, this phase enabled Karen to flex with the requirements of raising her family. This part of her career journey nurtured her home design interests.

Skills: construction worker sourcing and management, project management, customer design collaboration, project and scope definition, sales

6. Entrepreneur, CEO, Senior and Home Care Services

Karen Stephenson's latest venture and self-funded business investment harkens back to the many skills she accumulated in the course of her career. After much research, she joined another industry on the rise. With her children well on their way to managing their own lives, Karen engineered her next role. She helps the sandwich generation provide care for their parents and loved ones in their own homes through non-medical senior home care services.

The inevitable aging process and respective services to support independent lives for the elderly has stimulated a growing business trend. In her new business, Karen is an advocate for vulnerable elders and their family members. She is a spokesperson and educator for caregivers.

She manages a staff of over 130 workers and competes in a fractured services market of over four hundred agencies in Chicago. Because she has been in competitive positions for much of her career, Karen provides transparency and access to competitive analysis documents, enabling her customers to make informed choices.

For Karen, this project is mission driven. During this phase of her career, she is in search of meaning and purpose. Her social work skills are a valuable asset in her role as a senior care leader.

Skills: leadership, advocacy, business strategy, social media public service messages, business management, operations management, social service workers management, and, of course, sales!

Karen's journey through her career defines a series of projects launched in response to her professional desires and personal needs. She worked for larger companies offering training and operations infrastructure before buying her own business. I also observed Karen as she toggled part-time sales jobs on the side during her general construction days.

As a single woman, she established a legacy of drive and accomplishment. Her resourceful mentality and deliberate progress ensures eventual retirement, while she pursues her current project of purpose and meaning.

Her long list of Facebook followers can see she is surely optimizing creativity, growth, and happiness in her life's work.

If you are still not convinced a project frame of mind is for you, consider the rumbling already in play throughout the work landscape. You might want to ask yourself: How do I fit into the changing workplace? or How do I prevent myself from becoming obsolete?

The Next Big Wave of Change in the Workscape: Adapt or Become Extinct

We are in the midst of a shifting decade of transformation kicking the global workforce into action. Mass extinction of a significant portion of Fortune 500 companies is predicted in fewer than ten years. Here are some data points to support these startling predictions and estimates:

- In 2015, John Chambers, current executive chairman and former CEO of Cisco Systems, stated more than one-third of businesses today will not survive the next ten years. He contended many companies would fail at turning themselves into digital companies, spelling their demise.

- According to a study from the John M. Olin School of Business at Washington University, 40 percent of Fortune 500 companies on the S&P 500 will no longer exist in ten years.

- In 2011, Steven Denning, a leadership innovation consultant and longtime worker at the World Bank, made a dramatic statement in *Forbes*. He claimed the life expectancy of a Fortune 500 company had gone from seventy-five years (fifty years ago) to fewer than fifteen years today.

Creative destruction, where new ideas, technology, or infrastructure replaces outdated systems, is alive in the debris of obsolete companies like Kodak and Borders. Given their status as thriving enterprises, who thought their existence would decline so rapidly? Both companies failed to respond to consumer needs or make the technology changes necessary to survive.

Companies like Apple, Shutterfly, and Instagram have disrupted the way we capture and share photos. Digital expression replaced analog processes. Amazon's publishing arm and distribution efficiencies replaced the retail bookstore delivery model, spelling the demise of many retail outlets.

The financial industry is also witnessing a series of challengers to the status quo. New approaches to the markets such as Bitcoin and Blockchain (new forms of digital currency) are attempting to disrupt the current clearinghouse methods for financial transactions. These inventive concepts will change the way we finance innovation across the business landscape.

Nimble competitors will replace many Fortune 500 companies. Their fast growth and consumer product demand will feed the incessant shareholder appetite for sales and profits. The forces of creative destruction ensure we are better off through steady innovation and stimulation of the consumer-focused economy.

The Darwinian mantra grows in intensity. The message for organizations and working individuals is clear: adapt or become extinct.

Millennial Mobility and the Golden Age of Projects

Like the basics of chaos theory, when millennials flap their wings in one corner of the working stage, a string of events take place.

Among the many trends shaping the future of workers, the millennial generation is estimated to make up 75 percent of the workforce by 2025. Their increasingly mobile attitudes regarding job tenure and job preferences are shaping the workplace of the future.

A project mentality as a framework for job roles already exists within this generation. My interviews with millennials highlighted a few insights:

- They are mobile, leading to shorter tenure. Some analysts refer to this behavior as job hopping. Millennials are willing to move from an existing role if the job is not a good fit or does not challenge or engage them.

- They are comfortable with testing different types of roles for the purpose of comparison. This attitude is a reflection of the A/B testing approach discussed earlier and an indicator of a project mindset.

- They expect accomplishment within shorter timeframes

According to a study organized in 2016 through Millennial Branding, Identified.com, and the Orrell Group, only 7 percent of millennials work at large corporations. The study reviewed four million Facebook profiles to collect the data.

The millennial generation is threatening the existence of large companies by voting with their working feet. They have responded in great numbers by working at smaller companies, launching entrepreneurial businesses, and participating in the freelance economy.

While decreased job timeframes and shorter tours of duty reflect the habits and preferences of millennials, the ripple effect has broad impact across the multi-generational workplace. As described in the experiences of Karen Stephenson and Ric Dragon, shorter-term engagements are a practical response to change on the path of fulfilling work.

Project Runway

OK, this is a different project runway than the fashionista designer who wants to impress the judges on the TV show with the same name!

In the startup world, you will often hear company leaders say, "We have six months of runway," (or whatever number is relevant) before requiring additional investment. When hearing this phrase, all hands are on deck working to accomplish the goals of generating more revenue or gaining access to more capital.

There is a sense of urgency during this time. You may have heard the stories about startups performing brilliantly (pivots, new ideas, more sales) during this compressed schedule. Harnessing the energy provided by time constraints can produce amazing results.

The project runway range for an agile career role is two to three years.

Tapping into this bursty stream of productivity across all generations requires practical management of short-term employee engagements. Inherent in the new alliance between employers and employees is the effort from both sides to harness the benefits of employee engagement. The perks of employee engagement include: mutual trust, high performance, problem-solving attitude, job satisfaction, accountability, and happiness, among others.

Reasons to Believe: Iterative Careers and a Project Mindset

When you are making an important decision to choose one product or service over another, a salesperson will provide a list of features and benefits. Or you may be a *Consumer Reports* aficionado who researches every aspect of the product before you buy.

Let's take a look at some of the benefits of viewing job roles as projects. Many of these benefits are derived from the advantages of agile software development.

You Are the Navigator
Enables you to make decisions and changes, rather than someone making them for you.

Practical Time Constraints
Prevents you from getting into long and indefinite job cycles. These protracted periods block you from knowing what actually works for you and what does not.

Flexible Framework
Allows sufficient room for accommodating the new needs/ necessities and work preferences without disturbing the whole career. In complex careers, you may not have a concrete idea of what appeals to you and what it takes to get there. The iterative, project-based process is more flexible, as it allows for change.

Learning = Engagement
Offers a steep learning curve in the beginning and encourages engagement.

Fine-Tuning for Better Long-term Outcomes
Shorter-term engagements allow for course correction with each new role. The path to fulfilling work requires adjustments.

Diversified Portfolio
Just as an investment portfolio comprised of multiple opportunities reduces overall risk, testing your appetite for job preferences with a project mindset will encourage an all-in mentality as you make progress with each role. You are building a portfolio of experiences and competencies, increasing your value with each project step.

Project Completion Satisfaction

You complete a program or a project, demonstrating progress and adding milestones to your career portfolio.

Quality improvement

By breaking down the long-term view into manageable projects, you can focus on progress, test your ideas, and obtain input from your feedback squad, mentors, and advocates. By moving onto new projects with testing and reviews during each iteration, quality is improved. Similar to product development, you can find and fix defects quickly while identifying expectation mismatches early.

Increased Engagement

A shorter timeframe optimizes engagement potential. Think of when you started a new job or new role. Focus and motivation are high when starting something new.

Now that we've reviewed the features and benefits of project thinking, perhaps there is an enduring idea waiting for your project launch. A new job? A career shift? A side gig? A new business?

The Agile Careerist Project

Speaking of projects, a few years ago I launched the career agility idea as a project. Intrigued by the role of agile methods in the software development process, I wanted to dig deeper into the broader topic of agility.

What started out as a quest to fine-tune my evolving career sparked a research initiative. In the persistent swirl of change and competing employer-employee agendas, and true to the hearty suggestion defined by the *Pursue It in Parallel* principle in this book, I launched a side pursuit. I labeled it *The Agile Careerist Project.*

As a creative exploration and fact-gathering endeavor, the moniker of the project enabled me to explore its potential in the areas of research, a training platform, a blog, a business, a book, and beyond.

In particular, the chapter covering the principle Optimization of Your Personal Brand grew into a lovely detour where I helped people in my network define and explore their career brands. With two decades of design and corporate brand development experience as a reference point, the imperative of personal branding grew with each individual encounter. This relevant diversion also resulted in a combined career and brand map illustration guide—a useful sketch on the career navigation path.

Allowing this deliberate detour to capture my attention extended my circuitous agility research project by many months. Yet it resulted in extraordinary career insights. Just as Michael Porter, the renowned Harvard professor, researcher, and business author, defined five competitive forces for business, I uncovered worker competition forces. These forces of individual worker competition correlate to the seven principles in this book. One thing I know for sure is career branding tops the list of competitive forces for the individual careerist.

The Agility Project has now changed into a media and education company with a blog, a book, a career development model, and a series of career development workshops.

Project Name Game

In addition to the decision to launch a project, did you know there is a psychology to naming projects? A name reflects the personality and ambition of the project owner (that's you!) and often telegraphs the project vision.

Developers have been doing it for years. The formal names of the products we buy were once known by their code names. When working for technology companies, I worked on projects like Blackbird and Iguana. One of these code names belonged to a highly visible global computer enterprise and the other one belonged to a software company. Some code names stick and others are replaced by commercial brand names.

Why does this practice exist? The project owner can influence the brand of the project by establishing a humorous or badass persona, while inspiring the team to rally behind a vision.

While naming your next job role may not be top of mind, you certainly have the option to spice up your efforts by naming your side gig. Operation Adventure, Transformation Project, or Project Breakthrough are examples of potential names reflecting excitement about making a change.

When researching the name *Agile Careerist Project*, my goal was to express agility and the image of a vigilant and determined individual. I discovered several authors and organizations branding their projects with descriptive names. Their intentional use of the word "project" gave them scalable business flexibility as their efforts evolved. A few examples are:

Happiness Project – by Gretchen Rubin

Blog, book, movement, product company

The Good Life Project – by Jonathan Fields

Blog, books, movement, conference series, media enterprise, consulting company

52 Lists Project – by Moorea Seal

Blog series and journal for list lovers, a year of weekly journal inspiration

Wounded Warrior Project

A military and veterans charity service organization empowering injured veterans and their families

Whether you choose to honor your subsequent career venture with a name or transform your current gig into your next profession with the seamless ease of a magician, the decision to make a change starts with a vision. A project mindset may encourage you to create a role consistent with the talents of your champion efforts.

You Just Know

There are countless quotes about knowing when you've found the right one. What better way to end a chapter than with the classic search for what's right in our lives? Nora Ephron was a master scriptwriter, imagining the nuanced feelings and visceral reaction of "just knowing."

While this book is about our life's work and not necessarily about love, the timeless story about the search for meaning in our careers is a story rich with purpose and enduring emotion. Meister Eckhart said it best:

> And suddenly you know . . . It's time to start something
> new and trust the magic of new beginnings.
> —*Meister Eckhart, thirteenth century German theologian,*
> *philosopher, and mystic*

The Agile Careerist's Guide to the Galaxy

Congratulations! You have arrived at the final principle of your career navigation model. Make no mistake, however, adopting an agile mindset is an ongoing commitment to a long-term practice. Just like eating well, a meditation practice, or an exercise regimen, the agility muscle benefits from consistent use on your trek through the career landscape. Before moving on to the next steps, let's take a moment to view the simplified instructions for activating your agile career.

I encourage you to apply what is suitable for your life's work. The elements of change will continue to rotate within your work sphere, giving you ample time to test and explore these principles. The visual summary of the Agile Career serves as an InfoGuide of the seven principles for quick access.

The Agile Careerist Quick Guide

Agile Career Definition:

An agile career is a self-reflective, iterative career path guided by response to change, evolving job roles, and designed to optimize creativity, growth, and happiness.

Agile Career Principles:

1. **Create an Idea Zone.**

   Take a cue from software engineers. Develop an idea backlog or buffer zone for future use, like they do for software releases. Save the pixie dust of your creative genius by writing it down or creating a digital document for a rainy day when you are out of ideas, yet still want to make progress.

2. **Pursue It in Parallel.**

   Pursue side gigs, freelance work, consulting assignments, education, or hobbies. Create pathways for creative thought, extra income, or future job opportunities.

3. **A/B Test Your Career—Test and Measure.**

   Test your interest and aptitude as you say, "Which do I like better, Job A or B?" Move to Job C or go back to a role similar to Job A, depending on your track record or inclination. Give yourself permission to explore as you discover the best fit for you and your talents.

4. **Respond to Change.**
Acceleration of technology and continuous state of change calls for flexibility and willingness to adapt. Lean into change and make adjustments to your career status, rather than stick to a rigid plan. Acclimate to economic developments and corporate adjustments by uncovering engaging projects. Discover market and employment gaps you can fulfill in a unique manner.

5. **Optimize Your Personal Brand.**
Uncover your distinguishing characteristics or brand values. Package your portfolio of skills and be consistent in how you communicate and present yourself to the human workplace. Ask yourself, "Am I in alignment with my brand values?" Spread the story-driven message in real life and across your digital networks. Be bold and dare to be different.

6. **Activate the Feedback Squad.**
No one can do it alone. Seek the advice of people you most respect: mentors, trusted friends, and savvy colleagues. Hire a career coach. Learn from others via online channels. Pay it forward; be part of a feedback squad for a friend or coworker.

7. **Think of Your Career as a Series of Projects.**
Think of your work as evolving job roles. Consider two- to three-year projects capable of building on your incremental knowledge. Harness the enthusiasm of a fresh start, master the job, and build new

competencies. Become the most eligible employee for promotion or the best candidate at another company, or launch your personal startup project.

CAREER AGILITY MODEL

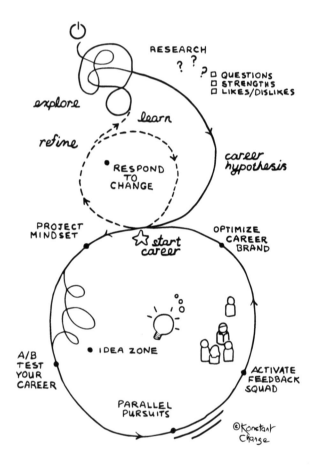

Now, let's get back to interactive part of the chapter. These exercises are designed to help you take control of forward intentional career movement, one project at a time.

Next Steps

With the mad skills of an expert project manager, breaking down long protracted blocks of time into smaller chunks makes life and work more manageable. Stringing together projects completes the full story of our goals and proud accomplishments.

The idea behind these exercises is to stimulate aspiration while simplifying practical steps to achieve what's possible in your career. Consider completing a couple of these exercises with the goal of identifying your next phase or career project.

Exercises

1. Understand where you've been and what you have accomplished in your life's work to create a blueprint for possibilities. Identify patterns, strengths, skills, and career progression in your career history.

   - As a guide, take a look at Karen Stephenson's distinct phases in her career and map out your career steps or phases.

   - Define the phases by looking at your resume or LinkedIn profile, or by referring to a career map created from an earlier chapter. As an example, you may have started out as an analyst or researcher and now you are a financial strategist working in mergers and acquisitions.

   - Elaborate on the phases or projects by classifying your job description and related skills.

- Document the patterns and your competencies in your work history through a one-page worksheet. There may be an obvious connector that ties it all together, or there may be a number of completely unrelated phases.

2. After identifying your skills and patterns, define a potential project or job opportunity on your radar. Create a few paragraphs outlining how your past projects support your current interest. This exercise is dependent upon completion of exercise number 1 above.

3. Analyze a specific project within your job role you launched or created where you derived a sense of accomplishment and pride. Define each of the steps necessary to accomplish the project.

4. Reach for the stars by listing three ideas or projects that attract your interest, yet may seem unlikely.

   - Explore and define the steps required for one option listed above to pursue this idea.

   - Referring to the project breakdown structure outlined in the space program example, write the steps necessary to achieve this goal (education, networking, career coaching, role positioning, etc.).

5. Seek insights from others. Meet with one person who appears to have stepped through their

career in a methodical way. Ask her how she moved from one segment of her career to the next. Take notes and define essential steps.

6. Add a dash of creativity to your work by naming your next project. Create a one-page description accompanied by milestones and tasks.

CHAPTER 9

Conclusion: Agile Careerist Mastermind

If you're in permanent beta in your career, twenty years of experience actually is twenty years of experience because each year will be marked by new, enriching challenges and opportunities. Permanent beta is essentially a lifelong commitment to continuous personal growth.
—REID HOFFMAN, FOUNDER OF LINKEDIN

The Agility Master Class

There are numerous thought leaders I discovered in my research. Like the movie *Julie and Julia*, where the author felt as though Julia Child was in the kitchen with her as she prepared the recipes, these agile influencers are daily muses for my body of work on career agility.

In addition to the many agility thinkers highlighted at the beginning of each chapter, the inspiration of agile thought leaders is never far from the winds of incessant change. Let's learn from the masters.

Continuous Learning

Reid Hoffman's relevant words regarding permanent beta guided me as I traversed the work landscape and researched the topics for this book. His groundbreaking work in the area of personal network development makes career agility possible.

The humble notion of continuous beta testing as a strategy for career progression challenges the know-it-all persona and paves the way for growth.

When studying and paying for college, I became addicted to achieving the milestone, the degree. Yet when college was over, the mile marker moved! Yes, the proverbial goal vs. the journey made me realize my work is never done. Aware that learning is never over and the movable mile marker translates to growth, I happily accept the role of perpetual student. Agility at its finest!

Adapt

> The more you adapt, the more interesting you are.
> —*Martha Stewart, entrepreneur, author, and television personality*

While my basic premise for career navigation is "adapt or get left behind," Martha Stewart's point of view spotlights a telling positive side effect of adaptable behavior. She came back from a seemingly insurmountable setback—a jail sentence for insider trading—yet she experienced rapid success as she took back the reins of her business.

Her journey from author of cooking, entertaining, and decorating books to lifestyle media maestro proved a sound training ground for nimble navigation in an evolving media environment.

"Adaptable" is an overarching theme for the successful agile careerist. Flexible people are easy to be around, to plan activities with, and to engage with on many levels. After all, who wants to be around an inflexible person who must have it their way?

When learning how to properly network in a crowded business event, we are frequently encouraged to listen more than talk. Asking questions is a good strategy. People find us more interesting and likable.

Now it's time to apply the adapt rule when building relationships. People may find you fascinating!

Continuous Transformation

> The only way you survive is you continuously transform into something else. It's this idea of continuous transformation that makes you an innovation company.
> —*Ginni Rometty, CEO of IBM, the first woman to head the company*

Although Ginni Rometty's quote refers to the business enterprise, continuous transformation applies to individual development and is another form of permanent beta. The dynamic nature of the business environment requires a responsive mentality poised to integrate just-in-time thinking.

Growing up in a modest single-parent household, she observed her mother's transformation from stay-at-home mom to college student to professional business manager. Transformation equated to taking control and being responsible for your family.

As one of the leading female technology geeks of our time, Ginni Rometty migrated through multiple tours of duty throughout IBM. She held roles in systems engineering, consulting, senior leader of sales/marketing/strategy, chairman, president, and CEO. While these positions are impressive, her geek status is highly revered by her peers and members of the technology community.

Response to Change, Adversity, and Circumstances

> Life is 10 percent what happens to you
> and 90 percent how you respond to it.
> —Lou Holtz, former American football player,
> coach, motivational speaker,
> and football analyst

Unexpected turns in a career are pervasive. Like unpredictable winter storms moving across the continent, the ultra-clear path we see today can be reduced to zero visibility at the whim of a management decision.

During a motivational speech by Lou Holtz, I witnessed his enduring belief regarding doing the best you can. As an inspirational leader, he believes motivation and attitude magnify capability. Teaching this on and off the field, his spirited response to challenges encourages others to persist, especially in the second half of the game.

When career change descends upon us without warning due to technology, economic shifts, politics, setbacks, and surprises, it's time to be a first responder. Our responses will set us apart from those succumbing to the situation, rather than taking action. What will be the mark of your 90 percent?

Test, Try, Fail, Measure

> You win by trying. And failing. Test, try, fail, measure,
> evolve, repeat, persist...
> —*Seth Godin, author, entrepreneur, marketer,*
> *and professional speaker*

Seth Godin's perspective is reflected in the "A/B Test Your Career" chapter, where you are encouraged to test different roles until you figure out what fits. Whether at the beginning of your career, mid-career, or at a plateau, giving yourself permission to test new roles opens up opportunities. You win by trying.

Over thirty years, Seth wrote twenty-four books (and counting). Many of his books introduce fresh ideas, providing the ideal platform for testing. By tracking how many people buy his books and write positive reviews, book publishing enables measurement. Failures are quickly identified and resources are reallocated for evolution of successful concepts.

A significant benefit of the test and measure approach takes away the pressure of having to choose only one track. Testing gives you the ability to breathe and explore. Take a deep breath ...exhale... E X P L O R E.

Work as a Calling

My Aunt Cele believed work was a calling.

While a resilient and feisty demeanor set her apart, it was her reverence for work that impressed me when I first hunted for employment. She encouraged me to form a positive relationship with my profession, especially helpful when certain early job experiences felt more harmful than good.

Reality Check

Let's get real. There are times when regardless of your attitude, the potholes in your career path turn into sinkholes.

One memory in particular left an impression: the time I got fired from an advertising agency. The job had not been a good fit from the start. I was told to pack up immediately and walk in the path of shame past fellow employees who alternately stared and looked down at the floor. Leaving the design studio with my scarce belongings, I could feel the heat of embarrassment rise up to my forehead.

Bruised egos and the curse of mismatched work environments are part of the roads frequently traveled through failed career experiments. The whole truth about work lies somewhere between a positive experience and an abandoned mistake.

Which brings me to one of the most valuable lessons of the agile career: responding to change may take a little longer! While interviewing individuals, they occasionally confessed a decision to stay with a job, in spite of the misalignment. Yes, there are times when it is reasonable and practical to extend your length of stay in a less-than-ideal role. This is one of my favorite quotes on the topic:

> Do what you have to do until you
> can do what you want to do.
> —Oprah Winfrey

One woman explained her strategy to wait two years to make a career shift, as she wanted to get her children through college with a solid salary before taking a potential financial risk. She did, however, continue to parallel her career change ideas on the side prior to making the change two years later.

Other workers talked about the responsibility of raising small children or the hindrance of a medical setback. These are all legitimate variables to consider in establishing a balanced career equation. There are many reasons for weathering the storm a while longer. The suggestion, however, is to make decisions guided by intention, rather than react with fear or caving in to the will of others.

Career Hierarchy

As demonstrated by Karen Stephenson and Ric Dragon in the "Think of a Career as a Series of Projects" chapter, their persistent search for meaningful work landed them in the enviable group of satisfied workers. Yet the search for meaning can be rerouted a few times before you get there. During Karen's career, she made sensible decisions to accommodate her personal circumstances, as she was raising two children.

Many career stories offered in earlier chapters illustrated the hierarchy of career needs. Even as we follow a plan or adopt a career navigation strategy, we make decisions based on our personal situations and needs.

Hugh MacLeod, a prominent cartoonist and business consultant, created an elegant career hierarchy illustration. The image mimics Maslow's Hierarchy of Needs diagram, a triangle that starts with basic human needs and results in self-actualization. Abraham Maslow was a twentieth century psychologist who developed a humanistic approach to psychology.

Hugh MacLeod's hierarchy diagram portrays the classic triangle, starting from paycheck to paycheck, project to project, and adventure to adventure. The reason his interpretation of work progression resonates with the masses is we often choose our careers in pursuit of money or take a job with the first employer who agreed to hire us.

Adventure-to-adventure in Hugh's illustration is the parallel idea to self-actualization in Maslow's Hierarchy. The diagram suggests that attaining adventure in our work makes us most happy and evolved in our careers.

CAREER HIERARCHY

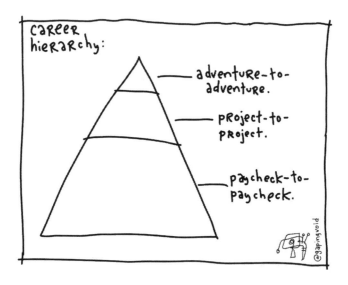

Now that we have learned from numerous agility masters, I will reinforce the main message of this book and share why I started the Agile Careerist Project.

Doing the Right Thing by Helping People Who Work

The main message of this book is, "Adapt to change, or get left behind." If you take away only one idea, this command outlines the serious requirement of career relevance in the workplace.

My reason for writing this book is to help you manage the entire continuum of your work experiences by following the principles outlined here. This is especially relevant when the current of change greets you with a challenge or a temporary defeat.

As part of the agile career definition provided earlier, an agile career is designed to optimize creativity, growth, and happiness.

My hope for you is to adopt an agile careerist mindset to help you accommodate change while taking iterative steps to achieve creativity, growth, and happiness in your life's work.

You've earned it.

Continue the Conversation re: The Future of Work

Wow! You are on the final pages of the book. Thanks for hanging out with me. You have my genuine appreciation for taking the journey with me and several agile careerists profiled in the book.

The website agilecareer.com offers a chance to join the community of agility thinkers as they respond to the future of work. Take a look at the *Idea Zone* to join. You will find more information on day-to-day strategies for creating movement and growth for your career.

Want to know more about expanding your network, the future of work, writing an effective resume, or creating or building your personal brand? You will also find additional online resources and tools, downloadable guides, and a useful Agility Meter (agility assessment tool).

Thank You

To my husband Bruce, who believed in me at the first mention of agile career, a topic that became my trusty companion for the next four years. He consistently shared my project and book concept with anyone who would listen, including the stranger sitting next to him on a plane.

To my developmental editor, Joann Dobbie, who challenged me to be a better writer, and my copy editor, Kim Bookless, whose meticulous and caring efforts turned this into a professional publication. And to my book designer Gwyn Snider, who translated my design brief into real art.

To my sister, Maureen Cannon, who signed up for proofreading years before the book was completed. She was the first person to read and proof the copy-edited manuscript.

To Jonathan Fields and The Good Life Project participants, who helped me distill an emerging idea into reality during the New York Entrepreneurial Alignment Lab.

To the team of agile marketers, especially Jim Ewel, Jasha Kaykas-Wolff, Kirstin Falk, Scott Brinker, and John Cass, with whom I collaborated in San Francisco to create the Agile Marketing Manifesto in 2012. While applying principles and values from agile software development to the discipline of marketing, a spinoff idea of career agility was born.

To my business coach, Laurel Donnellan, whose career coaching insights helped me access my inner artist through writing and creating the illustrations for this book. She helped me wrestle with and capture key career agility concepts.

To the many careerists, thought leaders, and influencers I interviewed during the research phase of the book. You cleared your calendar to have a meaningful conversation with an agility seeker.

To my many friends, colleagues, and family, whose consistent interest, kindness, and support fueled the perseverance necessary to complete my ever-expanding side project.

And most important, to you, the readers. I am grateful for your curiosity and willingness to learn.

Meet Marti

Marti Konstant is a career growth analyst and founder of *The Agile Careerist Project*. Her career path includes: artist, designer, technology marketing executive, and impact investor. What started out as a quest to fine-tune her evolving career sparked a research project, book, and workshops where future of work and career agility are central themes.

A persistent optimist and prolific photographer, she lives in Chicago with her husband.

With movement as her muse, she is a runner, hiker, and long walker.

agilecareer.com

Made in the USA
Lexington, KY
30 June 2018